W9-AQV-820

The
U.S.
TIRE
INDUSTRY
A History

TWAYNE'S EVOLUTION OF AMERICAN BUSINESS SERIES

Industries, Institutions, and Entrepreneurs

Edwin J. Perkins
SERIES EDITOR
UNIVERSITY OF SOUTHERN CALIFORNIA

The
U.S.
TIRE
INDUSTRY
A History

Michael J. French

BISHOP MUELLER LIBRARY

Briar Cliff College

SIOUX CITY, IA 51104

TWAYNE PUBLISHERS ☐ BOSTON
A Division of G. K. Hall & Co.

The U.S. Tire Industry: A History
Michael J. French

Copyright 1991 by G. K. Hall & Co.
All rights reserved.
Published by Twayne Publishers
A division of G. K. Hall & Co.
70 Lincoln Street
Boston, Massachusetts 02111

HD
9161.5
.T573
45443
1990

Copyediting supervised by Barbara Sutton.
Book design and production by Gabrielle B. McDonald.
Typeset in Aldus with Optima display type.
by Huron Valley Graphics, Inc. of Ann Arbor, Michigan.

The paper used in this publication meets the minimum requirements
of American National Standard for Information Sciences—Permanence
of Paper for Printed Library Materials, ANSI Z39.48-1984. ⊚™

Printed and bound in the United States of America.

Library of Congress Cataloging-in-Publication Data
French, M.J.

    The U.S. tire industry : a history / M.J. French.
       p.   cm. — (Twayne's evolution of American Business series ;
    TEABS 6)
    Includes bibliographical references and index.
    1. Tire industry—United States—History. I. Title. II. Series:
    Twayne's evolution of America business series ; no. 6.
    HD9161.5.T573U5443   1990
    338.4'767832'0973—dc20   90-4906
                                                               CIP

0-8057-9817-X (alk. paper). 10 9 8 7 6 5 4 3 2 1
0-8057-9818-8 (pbk.: alk. paper). 10 9 8 7 6 5 4 3 2 1

First published 1990.

21910482

For Roma and Nicholas

CONTENTS

ACKNOWLEDGMENTS

IN UNDERTAKING THIS STUDY I HAVE IN-
curred many debts. Mrs. Mary Chapman kindly permitted access to her
father's papers in the J. Penfield Seiberling Collection, and F. Seiberling
allowed me to consult the Frank A. Seiberling Papers. These two important
collections are held at the Ohio Historical Society in Columbus, Ohio. The
Society's archivist Gary Arnold was most helpful on my visits to Columbus. For the pre–1941 period I was able to draw on the archives of the
Goodyear, Goodrich, and Firestone companies and the collections of the
University of Akron's Archives Department. The latter has recently received deposits of company archives that I hope will provide scope for
further study of the industry. My researching was generously supported by
the Carnegie Trust for the Universities of Scotland and by the University of
Glasgow. Without their assistance the enterprise would have been impossible, and I am most grateful. The comments Ed Perkins, Tony Slaven, and
Tom Hart made on earlier drafts were most helpful. Dian and Ronald Green
deserve special thanks. The constant support from my parents has been
invaluable. All shortcomings are my responsibility. Parts of chapters 5 and
6 appeared in an article in *Business History Review* 60 (Spring 1986); I am
grateful for the editor's permission to draw on this material and for the
earlier encouragement to my work on the tire industry. My greatest debt is,
and remains, to Roma.

INTRODUCTION

FEW ASPECTS OF AMERICAN BUSINESS HIS-
tory have attracted as much interest as the automobile, yet the role of the
related industries and consequences of their relationship to the automobile
industry are rarely examined and the tire industry receives particularly
short shrift. It is a commonplace that the automobile's economic impact
owed much to its central position within a bloc of industries supplying
components as well as services for the car user. Nevertheless, historians of
the automobile tend to ignore tires. General studies often refer to the
proportion of rubber consumed in tires; some 80 percent during the 1920s.
But the object is to stress the significance of the automobile. More specialist
accounts note changing tire designs, such as the invention of pneumatic
tires, or occasionally name leading tire producers. Biographers of Henry
Ford refer to his vacation camping trips between 1918 and 1924 in the
company of Thomas Edison, the naturalist John Burroughs, and Harvey S.
Firestone. The last was a major supplier of tires to Ford. Otherwise the
supply of rubber, its processing, and the marketing of tires are considered as
unproblematic responses to the imperatives of automobile demand. Like its
product, the tire industry is assumed to be in operation, but distinctly
subordinate to the automobile.

In its own right, the tire industry can be taken as an embodiment of
industrial enterprise in the twentieth century and, in particular, of the
changing character and fortunes of the U.S. economy. The rapid growth of
automobile production and use provided a vast new market for tires. Tire
producers felt profoundly the impact of the transportation phenomena that
transformed America. The new road building and expansion of residential
areas in some cities during the 1920s foreshadowed even greater expansion
of the interstate highway system and suburbanization after World War II.
As car ownership became more widespread, many aspects of American
society came to rely on motoring and, thus, required tires. The use of
automobiles became commonplace for commuters, shoppers, salesmen,

churchgoers, and tourists as well as in the increasing variety of leisure activities. Buses, taxis, and trucks displaced railroads in both local and long-distance movement of passengers and freight. The introduction of container-ized shipping shifted additional freight onto the roads. Even the growth of commercial aviation created its own demand for specialized tires. Against this background of favorable opportunities, the tire industry's own technol-ogy, research, business strategies, and the character of particular markets are important examples of the complex forces that shape business activity. The industry's problems and reorganization in recent years are a central part of a broader shift in the international standing and competitiveness of American manufacturing.

The largest segment of the nineteenth-century rubber industry was the manufacture of footwear. In addition, there were many small companies producing an ever-widening range of general rubber goods. The general firms supplied mechanical belting, hoses, and electrical products as well as a variety of consumer goods. In the latter category, the industry developed the manufacture of bicycle and carriage tires. This modest sideline was given greater importance by the bicycle craze that swept Europe and the United States during the 1890s. This episode, although short-lived, brought into being several enterprises that were to become the leading tire firms of the twentieth century.

The bicycle era foreshadowed the industry's later adaptation to the automobile. The original solid tires proved a poor product and pneumatic tires were soon developed. The pneumatics themselves were difficult to fit and to change when they punctured. In response new tire and rim designs were devised. A similar sequence of events occurred with automobile tires in the early 1900s. The new demands of heavier and faster vehicles triggered major innovations in tire construction, including the adoption of patterned treads. These innovations enabled smaller firms, notably Goodyear and Fire-stone, to compete with the leading manufacturers of bicycle tires. In line with the automobile sector as a whole, tire manufacturing matured rapidly.

The tire industry improved its products through steady advances in design, materials, and production methods. There were also more funda-mental changes, such as the introduction of lower pressure tires in the 1920s and radial tires in the 1970s. Early automobile tires were hard, gray-white, and narrow. The black color became standard in the 1910s, although white sidewalls and white lettering are also common. After 1959, and par-ticularly during the 1970s, tires became flatter and wider. Tires not only looked different, but also lasted far longer. Average tire life improved rap-idly, especially in the 1900s, 1920s, and 1970s. In these decades the product was the most important element in the industry's fortunes. To a degree such progress was offset by the greater demands made by motor vehicles, which became heavier or longer and faster. The higher average speeds required better road holding and braking performance from tires, although better roads did contribute to better tire wear. Motorists perhaps developed higher expectations of their tires and regarded any problems uncharitably. Nonetheless, the relative infrequency of punctures represents one of the major contrasts between modern motoring and the early days of the automobile era.

Manufacturing technology affected the industry in various ways. The rubber industry of the nineteenth century relied on the factory system from the 1840s. The vital process of vulcanization, which made rubber products durable, required considerable use of heat. Footwear manufacture involved carefully regulated assembly operations. Tires also had to be assembled and vulcanized. Once reliable pneumatic tires had been developed, firms concentrated on improving the production process. In the 1910s and early 1920s tire manufacturing followed the trend of other U.S. industries toward more capital-intensive production. New machinery and close attention to the flow of materials and products increased efficiency, and management hierarchies proliferated. The precise timing of this shift to mass production is open to debate. The important "core" tire-building machines came into operation between 1909 and 1912, but other major innovations were not in place until the 1920s. Moreover, the hectic pace of expansion until 1920 often led to overcrowded factories in which management's coordinating role may have been more effective in theory than in practice. Nonetheless, technical changes increasingly disadvantaged smaller producers and consolidated the position of the larger firms, leading to a decline in the number of firms after 1920. In the 1970s and 1980s the switch to radial tires brought new and yet more capital-intensive technology and a further attrition among firms. It also signaled a watershed in the international character of the tire industry. From 1900 until 1970 U.S. manufacturers operated virtually unchallenged in their domestic market and spread their operations overseas. After 1970, however, American producers lost ground to European and Japanese rivals. The European firms, notably Michelin, were superior in the new radial tire technology, while the Japanese firms gained from the success of their automobile manufacturers who moved overseas through exports and direct investments. The weakening of the U.S. automobile producers compared to overseas rivals also had an impact on the tire suppliers. In a series of acquisitions, major U.S. tire firms passed into foreign ownership, and the tire industry assumed an increasingly global character.

An important aspect of the tire industry was the character of its markets. Tire demand was divided between automobile manufacturers who purchased original equipment tires for new vehicles and motorists who purchased replacement tires. These two sectors were very different. On the one hand, tire firms were confronted by a few powerful automobile makers, able to bargain closely; low prices were offered in return for large orders.

On the other hand, the replacement market consisted of numerous customers with different degrees of bargaining power as well as a variety of retail outlets. The emergence in tire retailing of mail-order and chain stores in the 1920s and oil companies in the 1930s confronted tire manufacturers with more powerful customers who demanded lower prices. The mass distributor, in turn, stimulated greater price competition in the replacement market. The two parts of the tire market were closely related in that replacement demand followed earlier original equipment (OE) sales. Weak OE sales could create excess capacity, which, in turn, increased competition in the replacement business. The tire industry faced the challenge of meeting both forms of tire demand. In this respect, the tire industry provides a good example of a sector where a high degree of producer concentration is offset by the structure of the final product markets.

The tire industry generally sought to avoid government involvement in its affairs. However, government has been an influence. In the 1920s industry and government cooperated in promoting U.S. plantation investment as an alternative to foreign control over the industry's basic raw material. During the 1930s the relationship was more uneasy. There were efforts to use the codes of the National Recovery Administration to control competition, but these failed. In the sphere of labor relations, the industry resisted the growth of labor unions. World War II saw an expansion of business-government cooperation with far-reaching effects on the tire industry. The synthetic rubber industry was created through federal finance and remained under federal control until 1955. Industry cooperated with government, but it was the pressure of war that led to the creation of synthetic rubber capacity and removed the dependence on imported natural rubber. Government defense contracts promoted greater diversification in the tire industry. During the 1960s the earlier distaste for government intervention resurfaced. The 1960s produced a new demand for some clear and uniform system of grading tire performance. The industry would have preferred self-regulation to the eventual federal standards, and there was also criticism of broader federal environmental legislation.

By the 1970s the industry faced fundamental changes. The advent of the more durable radial tires was accompanied by a decline in demand owing to recessions and the impact of higher oil prices. At the same time the American automobile manufacturers struggled in the face of sluggish domestic sales and superior overseas vehicles. The combined effect of these new elements was to intensify competition and to ensure that tire manufacturing and marketing assumed a global character. The emergence of oligopolistic competition within the U.S. market during the 1920s and 1930s was now paralleled by the emergence of a few major multinational producers. Several leading American firms were acquired by European and Japanese rivals, and by 1990 Goodyear, the only remaining major independent U.S. firm, was competing internationally with Michelin and Bridgestone. The revival of tire demand has benefited the industry, but its future appears to be a continuation of its balancing act between the influence, and attractions, of low cost, mass production, and the higher profit margins offered by the marketing of specialist or higher-value tires.

1

The Nineteenth-Century Rubber Industry

IN THE LATE EIGHTEENTH CENTURY A handful of Europeans became interested in an unusual liquid obtained from the bark of trees and vines in South America. When heated the milky fluid hardened into india rubber, or caoutchouc, a substance possessing elastic and waterproofing properties, which was used in making footwear and garments in the Amazon region. At first a curiosity, rubber's properties offered considerable potential, and early experiments led to small-scale commercial ventures. In 1811 J. N. Reithoffer established a business in Vienna. Thomas Hancock opened a London workshop in 1820. The products were simple: strips of rubber sewn into material formed garters and waistbands. In the United States of America a Boston merchant, Thomas C. Wales, imported rubber shoes from South America.

The first technical challenge was to render blocks of rubber workable. During the eighteenth century, French scientists had discovered that turpentine dissolved rubber, and in 1823 Charles Macintosh obtained a British patent for waterproofing cloth with a solution of rubber and coal tar. In 1820 Thomas Hancock patented a machine in which spiked rollers softened scraps of rubber. American interest lagged behind the Europeans until Edwin M. Chaffee, a foreman in a leatherworks, established a factory in Roxbury, Massachusetts, in 1828 to manufacture waterproof garments. The business flourished and was incorporated as the Roxbury India Rubber Company in 1833. Chaffee patented the "Monster," a calendering machine that used steam-heated rollers to press rubber into fabric. The Roxbury firm's initial success attracted other ventures, including Nathaniel Hayward's Eagle Rubber Company in 1835, and by 1837 there were about a dozen American manufacturers producing coats, caps, wagon covers, bags, footwear, and life preservers.

The fledgling industry was handicapped, however, by fundamental product weaknesses in its manufacturing technology. Solvents gave an unpleasant odor to the finished goods, while rubber solutions and mechanically processed rubber were both vulnerable to temperature change. Consequently, products became soft and sticky at high temperatures and brittle in cold weather, and the frequent return of unsatisfactory goods aggravated the normal financial difficulties of small producers in a new industry. There was little prospect of sustained growth without improved compounds, and several firms failed after the Panic of 1837, while the survivors were financially weakened.

The vital breakthrough was provided by the process of vulcanization invented by Charles Goodyear in 1839. Goodyear had followed his father into hardware retailing until illness and business failure resulted in the first of a series of imprisonments for debt. He had several patents to his credit and in 1833 sold an idea for an inflatable tube to Chaffee's Roxbury Company. This contact brought the industry's technical problems to Goodyear's attention, and he experimented with various rubber solvents before patenting a nitric acid process in 1837. Business success was elusive: a partnership with William Rider failed in the 1837 panic, and work with the Roxbury Company was halted by financial problems.

Goodyear began manufacturing in 1838 in the defunct Eagle Rubber plant, but both the products and the venture perished swiftly. Goodyear's experiments continued, and early in 1839 he discovered that a durable material was created when rubber, sulfur, and white lead were heated. After considerable further work, Goodyear patented the process of vulcanization on 15 June 1844; rubber, sulfur, and white lead heated to around 270 degrees Fahrenheit produced a compound that was flexible, impervious to water, and yet resistant to high and low temperatures. Two years later an Englishman, Alexander Parkes, devised a cold process of chemical vulcanization, which was particularly effective for gloves, balloons, and thin films of rubber. The two vulcanizing processes provided the technical foundation of rubber manufacturing.

Although an ardent publicist of the myriad possible uses of rubber, Goodyear's poor health, unstable finances, and preference for scientific work restricted his commercial activities. His patent position was strengthened by successful litigation against Horace H. Day's rival patent and the Patent Office's extension of Goodyear's patent in 1858. Several entrepreneurs took licenses under Goodyear's patents. His brother-in-law was among the investors who established the Naugatuck India Rubber Company (1844) and Goodyear Rubber and Packing Company (1846); other new ventures included Samuel J. Lewis and Co. of Naugatuck, Connecticut, a footwear business that later became the Goodyear Metallic Rubber Shoe Company. Early Goodyear licensees for general manufacturing included J. R. Ford and Co. (1848), William Rider (1848), and the Goodyear Rubber and Packing Company (1846). The latter was reorganized in 1856 by William Judson and John A. Cheever as the New York Belting and Packing Company and survived the burning down of its Connecticut plant in 1858.

Initially, Goodyear's patents exercised some control over the rate of entry of new firms into rubber production. This also held up profit margins in the early years. Consequently, while real value-added (sales minus costs) increased from $1,928,000 to $3,059,100 in the decade to 1859, there were still only 27 factories manufacturing rubber products. However, Goodyear's patents expired in 1865 and production and sales expanded particularly rapidly in the 1870s. By 1889 there were 167 plants employing 20,152 workers.

The principal division among rubber manufacturers was between those who specialized in footwear and those making a more general range of rubber goods. During the nineteenth century, boots and shoes were the industry's major product, and the footwear sector was dominated by large, highly capitalized firms. The 1889 census listed 11 specialist footwear manufacturers with an average workforce of 830 compared to an overall rubber industry average of only 121 workers. Patent licensing created the initial concentration in footwear production, but it was sustained by technical influences that promoted factory operations. Vulcanizing ovens imposed significant fixed costs, and the compounding and vulcanizing, or curing, processes required careful regulation. Equally, considerable dexterity was involved in assembling a boot or shoe, and the different sizes and designs limited the scope for standardization. The resulting reliance on skilled labor produced a clustering of rubber footwear factories in the traditional leather and shoe producing centers of Massachusetts and Connecticut, which also provided access to established wholesaling networks.

Demand for rubber footwear was highly seasonal, with the bulk of sales made late in the year in northern and upper-midwestern states. As a result, business was prone to drastic slumps during mild winters, when overstocked inventories triggered price cutting as producers and distributors tried to maintain sales. Such uncertainty encouraged successive attempts to establish price agreements. In 1848 six companies organized the Goodyear Associates and Licensees to set production quotas and prices, and, after Goodyear's patents lapsed, the nine members of the Associated Rubber Shoe Companies discussed prices between 1865 and 1886. However, profitable operations attracted new entrants in the late 1880s. By 1890 the footwear sector had three tiers: the combined sales of the three leading firms accounted for nearly half of total sales, a group of four medium-size firms supplied a quarter of total output, and ten small firms were responsible for the remaining quarter of sales.

Since even the smallest firms could influence prices and demand depended so much on seasonal climate, trade was inherently unstable. Following the collapse of a price agreement, financial interests promoted a rubber footwear trust as a device to reduce capacity and competition, a tactic used in many other industries. In 1892 Charles Ranlett Flint, a merchant and financier with interests in rubber importing, combined 11 companies through a series of stock options to create the United States Rubber Company, which controlled half of footwear sales. The constituent firms manufactured on a commission basis for a central selling organization supervised by a board of directors, but in practice the individual units retained virtual autonomy. The trust closed two small plants and extended its market share to 75 percent by 1898 through the acquisition of its principal rivals, Woonsocket Rubber Company (1893) and Boston Rubber Shoe Company (1898). Yet profits were modest because surviving independents and new entrants maintained competition. The trust's resources were strained by its strategy of absorbing rivals, and although Flint claimed savings on overhead costs, the trust's loose structure militated against major economies on labor or materials, the principal expenses.

The 1889 U.S. Census identified 11 plants specializing on belting and hose and 139 "other rubber goods" factories that manufactured a wide range of producer and consumer goods. Rapid industrialization in the late nineteenth century provided an increasing demand for mechanical goods, such as transmission belting and steam packing, while the sustained growth of railroad traffic promoted sales of springs, steam and brake hose, and buffers. Specialist belting and hose producers supplied such capital goods and formed part of the expanding machinery and engineering sector of the economy. By the 1880s, the introduction of electrical power was creating new markets for rubber insulation, and general economic growth and rising incomes stimulated demand for miscellaneous rubber products such as combs, toys, balloons, clothing, and medical and dental supplies. Belting required large calenders to impregnate fabrics with rubber, but other products involved a small, unskilled workforce using relatively simple equipment such as hand presses or performing relatively simple maneuvers such as dipping shapes into tanks of rubber solution. The vital skilled tasks of compounding and vulcanization were often performed by the factory superintendent who might be a partner or the full owner of the business.

General rubber manufacturers were principally located close to the wholesale markets in New York and New Jersey. In 1870 one tiny business made the first significant move away from the industry's East Coast origins and provided the foundations of the rubber industry in Akron, Ohio, the center of rubber manufacturing in the first half of the twentieth century. Dr. Benjamin Franklin Goodrich, a Civil War surgeon and real estate dealer, and John P. Morris had acquired the Hudson River Rubber Company in 1869 and a factory in Melrose, New Jersey. The firm's finances were weak, and Morris felt there was too much competition, so Dr. Goodrich sought a new location and additional capital. The doctor's travels included Jamestown, New York, and possibly Cleveland before he visited Akron, Ohio, where the local board of trade wished to attract new firms. Colonel George T. Perkins, president of the board of trade, inspected the Melrose plant, and in 1871 a group of Akron businessmen contributed $13,600 in loans to finance a new venture—Goodrich, Tew and Company. The Melrose machinery was shipped to Akron, and the company began production of belting and fire hoses.

The original partnership was dissolved and replaced by B. F. Goodrich and Company in 1874. When the initial loan fell due the following year, Colonel Perkins guaranteed its credit up to $35,000. But other business losses forced his withdrawal in 1878. Complete failure of the company was averted by support from George W. Crouse, another Akron entrepreneur. Crouse directed the incorporation of the B. F. Goodrich Company on 1 May 1880 with capital of $100,000, increased to $200,000 two years later. The reorganization provided much-needed financial stability and eliminated two of the partners, Benjamin T. Morgan and Henry F. Wheeler, who had fallen out with Goodrich and Crouse. In 1879 Alanson Work was appointed factory superintendent, and although he died from typhoid malaria in October 1881, his improvements to the firm's internal structure and manufacturing methods were vital to its revival. Sales rose from $319,358 to $695,979 between 1881 and 1888, while the workforce increased from 55 to 260. In 1882 Goodrich formed the Summit Rubber Company to manufacture hard rubber goods; this venture was absorbed by the firm three years later and reorganized as the B. F. Goodrich Hard Rubber Company in 1888. By this date the firm was sufficiently well established to survive Dr.

Goodrich's retirement and death. Several other midwestern producers had developed, notably Erie and Lake Shore Rubber Mills, Cleveland Rubber Works, Chicago Rubber Works, and Morgan and Wright.

☐ The Bicycle Tire Era

In the 1870s the rubber industry added a new line: bicycle tires. Cycling originated in France where the "velocifere" (1791) and the "draisienne" (1817) had enjoyed brief popularity. Both were simple frames with wooden wheels, which, lacking pedals, were pushed along with the feet. A renewed and more significant interest developed in the 1870s with the introduction of the "boneshaker" and then the "high-wheel" or "ordinary" bicycle. Despite its massive front wheel and tiny rear one, the "ordinary" popularized cycle racing and advanced bicycle design by using iron frames and being powered by pedals on the front wheels. In the 1880s manufacturers devised smaller, more manageable "safety" bicycles as well as tricycles and quadricycles. The "safety" bicycles embodied modern bicycle design with their use of tubular steel frames, wire spokes, ball bearings, chain drives, differential axles, and gears. Such innovations broadened the appeal of cycling, and Europe and the United States experienced a brief bicycle craze in the 1890s.

The American bicycle industry was pioneered by Albert A. Pope, who first imported English machines and then, from 1878, purchased bicycles from the Weed Sewing Machine Company of Hartford, Connecticut. Pope's imaginative marketing triggered an expansion of U.S. production from 12,000 cycles in 1881 to 40,000 in 1890. Pope also acquired bicycle patents, and until he lost his strong patent position in 1886, new entrants were discouraged. In 1890, Pope purchased the sewing machine company and developed an innovative business supplying high-quality cycles, while at the same time establishing the Hartford Cycle Company to supply cheaper machines. The Pope interests were a major element in a dramatic expansion of U.S. bicycle production to 1.2 million machines in 1896, in spite of a domestic recession. The surge in demand encouraged new entrants from the New England engineering trades and the rise of a midwestern bicycle industry, notably the Western Wheel Works in 1890. The bicycle craze created a tire business within the rubber industry.

On the "ordinary" bicycle of the 1870s, the rider's comfort was improved by strips of hard rubber cemented onto the metal channels around the wheel rims. Previously, wooden wheels were simply encircled by iron hoops or bands. Solid tires were relatively simple extensions of existing mechanical rubber goods, though there were difficulties in attaching the tires satisfactorily to withstand the strains of cycling. The initial popularity of cycling arose despite its discomforts, but wider interest, greater safety, and the racers' desire for speed all depended on improvements in suspension and handling. A key aspect was the wheel's contact with the ground, which determined steering and braking and the rider's general well-being. Solid rubber tires provided some relief, but the eventual solution was the pneumatic tire.

The idea of an inflatable tube predated the bicycle era and was first patented in 1846 in London by Robert William Thomson, a Scottish railway engineer. In an extraordinarily perceptive design, Thomson proposed an "aerial wheel" consisting of rubber or gutta-percha, inflated through a valve, and placed inside a leather cover. He envisaged tires being used on carriages, railroad wagons, and steam-driven road vehicles, but the inventive design was never implemented. Thomson, who patented a solid rubber tire in 1867, pursued a conventional engineering career, and carriages continued to use iron tires and to rely on wooden or iron springs for their suspension.

By the 1880s, the commercial environment had changed radically: rubber manufacturing was thriving, and bicycles and tricycles had established a market for solid tires. The sudden growth of cycling gave rise to a host of patents in the 1880s and 1890s. Cushion tires—little more than hollow rubber tubes fixed to the wheel rim—were introduced as an alternative to solid rubber tires and inventors devised all kinds of means of holding tires in place. The major advance, however, was John Boyd Dunlop's invention of a pneumatic tire in 1888.

Dunlop, another Scot, was a veterinary surgeon in Belfast who wished to improve the tires on his son's tricycle. He devised an inflated rubber tube enclosed by a cover of rubberized canvas: strips of canvas were wrapped around the tube and between the spokes of the bicycle wheel to hold the tire in place. Dunlop patented his pneumatic tire in 1889 and became a shareholder in Pneumatic Tyre and Booth's Cycle Agency Ltd., which was established in Dublin to market the tires. By holding air under pressure the pneumatic tire cushioned the impact of the road and, by reducing friction, made cycling less strenuous. Once demonstrated in cycle racing, the penumatic tire's greater comfort and speed ensured rapid acceptance. Dunlop's patent claims were undermined as early as 1890 by the rediscovery of Thomson's 1846 patent so the principle of the penumatic tire was readily available. Dunlop left the new firm in 1895, but the business prospered through the purchase of other major patents and effective marketing under the direction of the DuCros family.

Pneumatic tire design advanced swiftly around 1890 as inventors responded to the problems posed by cycling. Dunlop originally assembled each tire and wheel as a single unit, thus making the tire difficult to remove or repair, a severe drawback given the frequency of punctures. Innovations concentrated on the related problems of separating the inner tube from the casing, finding new methods of fixing the tire to the wheel, and improving valves. Amos Thomas of Philadelphia patented an inflatable single-tube tire, and in 1890 the idea, adapted from solid tires, of placing wire rings in the casing to grip the wheel rim was applied to pneumatics by Charles K. Welch in Britain and by A. T. Brown and G. F. Stillman in the United States.

A further advance was the clincher rim patented in 1890 by William Bartlett, the American manager of the North British Rubber Company in Edinburgh. Clincher tires were patented in the United States in 1891 and 1892 by Thomas B. Jeffrey, a pioneer bicycle maker, and became the standard cycle tire design. The clincher design changed the previously straight wheel rim into an inward curve and widened the base or bead of the casing so that it fit in the slot under the rim. The fitting and removal of tires was simplified further by changing the flat cross section of the rim into a hollow or drop-center design. The bead of the casing could then be more easily forced inside the rim. In 1893 Pardon W. Tillinghast patented a single-tube tire, and John Fullerton Palmer obtained American and British patents for a cord tire in which friction was reduced by using a fabric without cross-threads. The sequence of innovations enabled tires to be fixed in place firmly without becoming virtually impossible to remove and thus ensured rapid acceptance of pneumatic tires; by 1891 40 percent of new American bicycles were equipped with pneumatic tires, and within two years they were standard.

☐ Tire Manufacturing

Although the New England rubber footwear firms were located near the early centers of bicycle making, they ignored tires because their expertise had little in common with the new product. Tires consequently became the province both of new companies established to exploit patents and of existing general rubber goods firms, which added tires to their other lines. In contrast to the later automobile industry, several leading cycle makers integrated tire production with their firms. The Pope cycle interests acquired the neighboring Hartford Rubber Works in 1892; the rubber company had supplied tires for Pope's cycles since

1885. The Remington Arms Company added bicycles to its main business and manufactured tires under Bartlett's clincher patent. More influential was the Gormully and Jeffrey Manufacturing Company, a leading cycle maker, which, like Pope, later built automobiles. Jeffrey's clincher patent established precedence over Bartlett's claims in the United States, although positions were reversed in Britain. Gormully and Jeffrey used this key patent right to license other manufacturers as well as to market its own tires.

Dunlop's tire patent exercised no legal influence, but the firm did enter the U.S. market. Initially, an American producer was licensed, but in 1893 the DuCros established the American Dunlop Tire Company with a factory in New York. However, the business and all American rights were sold to the firm's Canadian manager in 1898. The firm's sale contributed to financing the parent company's transition from an assembler of tire parts to a full-line manufacturer in Britain. Dunlop did not return to the American market until after World War I.

Many general rubber manufacturers added tires to their established business during the 1880s, and they became more involved in the next decade when the bicycle craze coincided with a recession in other markets. Morgan and Wright was founded in Chicago in 1883 to manufacture rubber stamp gum and developed a varied range of cheap rubber goods before being transformed by the introducton of a double-tube pneumatic tire in 1891. Within five years, Morgan and Wright's daily output exceeded 8,000 casings with a range of 20 styles and weights; the firm was the leading independent tire producer. Most general firms relied on patent licenses and were rarely innovative in tire design but contributed to improving manufacturing methods. New York Belting and Packing sold $300,000 worth of tires in 1891–92 and installed additional machinery to meet demand. B. F. Goodrich was already supplying bicycle tires by 1888; it switched to pneumatics and expanded its tire department in 1892. Goodrich was licensed under Palmer's cord tire patents and Tillinghast's single-tube tire patent. In 1898 the firm constructed a new tire department and acquired Palmer's American rights and patents. Other general rubber firms to manufacture tires were Hodgman Rubber, Newton Rubber Works, Boston Woven Hose, the Mechanical Fabric Company, Columbia Rubber Works, Kokomo Rubber, Indianapolis Rubber, and Diamond Rubber. The last started life as Sherbondy Rubber in Barberton near Akron with financial support from Ohio Columbus Barber, president of the Diamond Match Company. The new firm initially supplied drug sundries, but expanded into tire manufacture. In 1894 it was renamed Diamond Rubber and then reorganized with new management and increased capital in 1898.

The success of Goodrich and Diamond Rubber prompted another Akron entrepreneur, John F. Seiberling, to enter the tire industry. Seiberling had been among the original investors supporting Goodrich's move to Akron and his own business interests encompassed milling, farm machinery, banking, and real estate. In 1895 three Seiberling cousins formed the Peoria Rubber and Manufacturing Company, and in the following year Seiberling established the Akron India Rubber Company. Within a year Seiberling encountered severe losses in his other ventures and sold the rubber business for $230,000 in 1898. However, his sons, Frank and Charles, started a new firm, Goodyear Tire and Rubber Company, that same year.

Goodyear Tire and Rubber began with paid-in capital of $43,000 raised by the Seiberling family, plus Henry Robinson, David E. Hill, and George Hill, three Akron businessmen, whose main interests were in clay products companies. Goodyear began with 13 workers using second-hand machinery in an abandoned strawboard factory. The firm's products included rubber horseshoe pads, rubber bands, and billiard cue tips, but tires accounted for over 80 percent of sales by 1900.

Bicycles provided the largest and most innovative tire market, but solid rubber tires and pneumatic tires became increasingly common on carriages during the 1890s. The solid tires were attached to the wheel rims by wires. The principal carriage tire design was patented by Arthur W. Grant and Edwin S. Kelly who formed the Rubber Tire Wheel Company of Springfield, Ohio, in 1894 to license manufacturers. In 1899 Rubber Tire Wheel was reorganized as Consolidated Rubber Tire. The following year, in anticipation of the Grant patent's expiration, Consolidated Rubber established an Akron factory operated by a subsidiary, Buckeye Rubber. The business later became Kelly-Springfield. Since Ohio, notably Cincinnati, was a center of the light carriage trade, and thus a major source of tire demand, the state's rubber firms benefited from the new market.

The bicycle trade flourished after 1891 and by 1896 production totaled 1.2 million machines. By 1897 American bicycle tire output was estimated at 3 million tires from a workforce of 3,000. This trade was significant in the expansion, aided by a cyclical upturn after 1896, of the "other rubber goods" sector. However, sales then slumped to 500,000 bicycles in 1898, and bicycle makers and tire producers cut prices and profit margins in the face of excess capacity. Although output revived to 1.2 million machines in 1899, the value of bicycle tire sales declined from $26 million to $11.2 million between 1898 and 1900. This contraction coincided with unprecedented merger activity throughout U.S. manufacturing as capital-intensive industries reacted to excess capacity and took advantage of opportunities for financial promotions in a stock market becoming more interested in industrial shares.

The bicycle trade differed slightly since it had prospered during the general depression of 1893 to 1895, and many general rubber firms chose to scale down their tire departments rather than seek to limit competition through a trust or cartel arrangement. Nonetheless, merger mania was evident. In 1892 Charles Ranlett Flint, then organizing the U.S. Rubber Company, was approached by August Belmont, a major financier with interests in New York Belting and Packing, with proposals for a trust combining mechanical rubber goods firms. Flint brought together five companies to form the Mechanical Rubber Company: New York Belting and Packing, Stoughton Rubber, Cleveland Rubber, Chicago Rubber Works, and the Fabric Fire Hose Company. Unlike U.S. Rubber, the Mechanical Rubber Company had little impact on the market. More fundamental change followed the collapse of bicycle sales.

In 1899 American Bicycle Company was created by combining 45 bicyclemakers accounting for 75 percent of the U.S. market. The bicycle trust proved an overcapitalized and short-lived product of the turn-of-the-century merger movement, and it failed in 1902. A more significant development in 1899 was the Rubber Goods Manufacturing Company (RGM). This trust was based on the Mechanical Rubber Company, but to it were added four more mechanical goods firms: Peerless Rubber, Sawyer Belting, Peoria Rubber, and the India Rubber Company. RGM established itself as the leading tire producer by obtaining 75 percent of the capital in Morgan and Wright and by purchasing outright the Hartford Rubber Works, American Dunlop Tire Company, Single Tube A and B Company, and Indianapolis Rubber. This impressive collection included all of the major bicycle tire producers and trade names, and it encompassed midwestern and East Coast markets. RGM held rights to the Tillinghast and Gormully and Jeffrey patents, the two principal American tire patents, giving it a powerful competitive advantage. The only surviving independents of note were Goodrich and Diamond Rubber in Akron. Yet RGM's position proved far from impregnable as tire demand changed profoundly in the new century.

Apart from defensive mergers, declining bicycle sales encouraged greater interest in the nascent automobile industry. Automobile technology originated in Germany and France, the first American gasoline automobile being made by J. Frank and Charles E. Duryea in 1893. Bicycle makers, such as Pope, Jeffrey, and Alexander Winton, as well as carriage builders, made automobiles, and their tire suppliers responded to the new demand. The Pope Manufacturing Company initiated the production of electric and gasoline vehicles in 1897, and the Winton

Motor Carriage Company was established in the same year. By 1899 there were 30 firms producing a total of 2,500 vehicles. Output consisted of a mix of steam, electric, and gasoline automobiles. There was a rough divide between New England firms supplying electric and steam-powered machines and midwestern companies concentrating on gasoline engines.

The early vehicles generally used solid rubber tires adapted from carriage tires, but Michelin pioneered pneumatic tires in a Paris-to-Bordeaux race in 1895. The French firm maintained a technical lead over the next decade. Hartford Rubber Works supplied tires to the Duryea brothers in 1895. The first pneumatic tires for a commercially produced automobile in the United States were manufactured by Goodrich in 1896 for Winton, who was based in Cleveland. Hartford Rubber Works supplied tires for Pope's automobiles from 1897. Diamond Rubber and Goodyear initiated automobile tire production in 1899. Automobile tires were expensive and, thus, an attractive prospect as the bicycle craze passed, but at the turn of the century, tire sales were dwarfed by sales of the rubber industry's traditional products: footwear, belting, and hoses.

Nonetheless, the bicycle era of the 1890s paved the way for change. Bicycle makers advanced elements of mass production through their use of interchangeable parts, coordination of production flows, and the technology of sheet steel stamping. By promoting a means of individual travel, the bicycle was, in historian David Hounshell's words, a "transitional" technology, which aided the emergence of the automobile. Equally, the 1880s and 1890s were a transitional phase for the rubber industry. The bicycle boom was too brief and footwear sales too large for the rubber industry to be fundamentally altered, but bicycle tire demand produced new firms, the introduction of the pneumatic tire, and manufacturing expertise that responded to the transforming effects of the automobile revolution.

2

The Beginning of the Automobile Era, 1900–1909

THE LEGACY OF THE 1890S WAS A NAR-rowly based tire industry dominated by Rubber Goods Manufacturing Company (RGM) with Goodrich and Diamond Rubber the only sizable independents. There were a few recent entrants, such as Goodyear, Pennsylvania Rubber, and Fisk Rubber, plus an unknown number of general rubber companies making tires on a small scale. U.S. Rubber, the footwear trust, had ignored tires. The new century began unpromisingly with the collapse of bicycle production and increasing competition in the carriage tire trade; it also saw the beginnings of a rapid shift into automobile tire manufacture, which was to transform the rubber industry. In the process, firms had to tackle the technical challenges presented by switching from bicycle and carriage to motor tires.

The first influence was a slump in bicycle output from 1 million machines in 1900 to only 225,000 in 1904, with the decline continuing until 1909. This devastating contraction destroyed the American Bicycle Company and prompted tire manufacturers to cut prices and to introduce lower-quality brands. The scale of the change is evident in the composition of Goodrich's sales: bicycle tires formed 40 percent of the value of company sales in 1900, declining to 23 percent in 1903 and only 5.3 percent in 1907. Tillinghast's single-tube tire patent had been used by RGM to license manufacturers and establish minimum prices, but declining demand swept such practices away. New firms challenged patent restrictions. In 1900 Goodyear expanded sales with cheap tires and successfully defended itself against an alleged breach of its Tillinghast license. RGM then withdrew the firm's license. Faced with the loss of its major product, Goodyear devised a slightly different manufacturing process for cycle tires and withstood a legal challenge from RGM in 1902. The episode accentuated price competition, and although Tillinghast's patent was upheld in a suit against the Continental Rubber Works in 1910, its influence dwindled in line with bicycle tire sales.

The carriage tire market also became more competitive. The Grant patent had been used carefully and profitably to control entry and to establish sales quotas and prices while the patent's owners, the Rubber Tire Wheel Company, had acquired many competitors. Grant's patent expired in 1902, however, and prices fell sharply in 1903 with the encouragement of carriage builders seeking lower costs in their own increasingly competitive trade. Although 18 firms tried to reestablish price and output agreements, control was impossible without the foundation of a recognized patent. Carriage tires were a central element in the formation of another small Akron business in 1900, Firestone Tire and Rubber Company. Harvey S. Firestone was a salesman in Chicago for the Columbus Buggy Company until the firm failed in 1896. He then formed his own carriage tire jobbing company; tires were purchased from Morgan and Wright and mounted on carriage wheels. Within two years Firestone had acquired one of his local competitors, but he was bought out, in turn, by the Rubber Tire Wheel Company as part of the creation of the Consolidated Tire Company. After a brief period with the new firm, Firestone became manager of a carriage tire department established by Whitman and Barnes, a drill and machinery firm, in Akron. As the center of the farm machinery trade followed the wheat frontier west, Whitman and Barnes were seeking new outlets. When their small venture into tires petered out, Firestone remained in Akron and, in 1900, a new buggy tire business, Firestone Tire and Rubber Company, was based on James A. Swinehart's "sidewire" method of attaching solid rubber tires. In 1900 Swinehart contributed his patent, and two of his partners invested $10,000 in the enterprise, while Harvey Firestone provided another $10,000. The sidewire tires were actually manufactured by Whitman and Barnes, and Goodrich. Firestone purchased Whitman and Barnes's branches in New York, Chicago, and Boston, opened new outlets in St. Louis and Philadelphia, and obtained agencies in other cities. It built up a good business supplying solid rubber tires for carriages and commercial vehicles. Swinehart left in 1902 to promote his tire in Europe but returned two years later to form the Swinehart Tire and Rubber Company producing solid tires in Akron. Meanwhile Firestone increased the firm's capital to $200,000 with significant financial backing from Will Christy, a local businessman involved in construction, banking, and a telephone company. With the ending of the Grant patent, Firestone moved from distribution into manufacturing by opening a small factory in 1903 to work up supplies of prepared rubber and fabric purchased from Goodrich.

The greater competition in bicycle and carriage tire markets encouraged interest in nontire lines. Most of the 14 rubber manufacturers established between 1900 and 1904 favored mechanical rubber goods, such as transmission belting or hoses. Existing firms also expanded sales of these lines as well as turning to new products. Goodrich added golf balls in 1902 and footwear in 1905; Diamond Rubber increased sales of steam packing, insulated wire, and hard rubber goods; and Goodyear began producing pharmaceutical sundries, golf balls, and rubber tiling. Although such diversification cushioned the impact of declining bicycle sales, of greater significance was an expansion of tire demand from the automobile and motorcycle industries. Many small firms assembled vehicles from parts purchased from suppliers, and automobile designs abandoned their early carriage and buggy styles. By 1904 the gasoline internal combustion engine had triumphed over steam and electric rivals because of greater reliability, power, and convenience. Table 2.1 outlines the automobile industry's spectacular growth.

The divide between new car production and current vehicle registrations was reflected in a separation between original equipment (OE) tires sold to automobile manufacturers and replacement sales to motorists. The trend in OE demand corresponds to new car sales and can be employed to estimate total tire demand as in Table 2.2. The numbers in Table 2.2 should be viewed as minimums since early tires wore rapidly and were replaced relatively more frequently than in later years. In the

Table 2.1. Passenger Car Sales and Registrations, 1901–9

	Factory Sales	Index (1905 = 100)	Registrations	Index (1905 = 100)
1901	7,000	29	14,800	19
1903	11,235	46	32,950	43
1905	24,250	100	77,400	100
1907	43,000	177	140,300	181
1909	123,990	511	305,940	395

Source: Flink, *America Adopts the Automobile, 1895–1910*, (MIT Press) 58, table 1.1.

Table 2.2. Estimated Unit Sales of Automobile Tires, 1901–9

	New Car Sales	OE Tires[1]	Total Tire Sales[2]
1901	7,000	28,000	96,552
1903	11,235	44,940	154,966
1905	24,250	97,000	334,483
1907	43,000	172,000	593,103
1909	123,990	495,960	1,710,207

1. OE tires estimated on the basis of four tires per vehicle.

2. Total tire sales calculated by assuming a constant relationship between OE and total sales. The relationship of OE to total sales averaged 29 percent from 1910 to 1917, a phase of growth comparable to that between 1900 and 1909.

Source: Flink, *America Adopts the Automobile, 1895–1910* (MIT Press).

early 1900s average tire life was only a few hundred miles compared with 2,000 in 1905 and 3,000 by 1910. Also implicit in the figures in Table 2.2 is the increasing demand for inner tubes. In addition to cars, output of motorcycles rose from only 160 machines in 1900 to 18,600 in 1909; the production of commercial vehicles (trucks) created a further tire market.

Passenger automobiles quickly became by far the largest and most influential source of derived demand for tires. The estimated 1.7 million automobile tires sold in 1909 were well below the 3 million bicycle tires sold in 1897, but car tires were larger and more expensive. Consequently, in 1904 the automobile tire and tube business was valued at $5.8 million compared with the $3.7 million sales of bicycle and motorcycle tires. By 1909 the automobile tire market had expanded to $33 million, while bicycle and motorcycle tire sales were only $4.5 million. The changing composition of tire demand was evident at the company level. In 1902 bicycle tires formed 25 percent and solid tires for carriages and motor vehicles 7 percent of Goodrich's total sales, but by 1907 automobile tires provided 33 percent of sales and cycle tires only 5 percent.

The growth of new tire markets altered the structure of the tire business. RGM shared the fate of many turn-of-the century trusts; although still a leading firm, its market share declined gradually. Then in 1905 U.S. Rubber acquired RGM in order to gain access to the tire sector, and in one step the footwear trust became the leading tire producer. Initially, the various elements of RGM operated independently. Morgan and Wright moved from Chicago to Detroit and was, thus, well located to serve the burgeoning automobile industry. The only other footwear specialists to enter tire manufacture were the Converse Rubber Shoe Company (1908) and Hood Rubber (1912).

Goodrich was well placed in the automobile tire business and expanded its market share from around 15 percent in 1904 to 21 percent four years later. Diamond Rubber achieved a similar growth rate from a lower base, and the International Automobile and Vehicle Tire Company was also prominent. A potentially influential new entrant was Michelin, through the acquisition of International Automobile and Vehicle Tire and the establishment of a factory in Milltown, New Jersey, in 1907. The French company's early superiority in automobile pneumatic tire design and production offered a major advantage, but the pace of American innovation in pneumatic tire design swept away Michelin's advantage just as the company opened its factory. Michelin's American subsidiary continued until 1930, but it was never a major force. Among the smaller tire specialists in 1900, Fisk Rubber accounted for 7 percent of automobile tire sales by 1908, while Goodyear's market share expanded from 2 percent to 5 percent between 1902 and 1909. Firestone began manufacturing tires in 1903 and had gained 6 percent of the market within six years. The smaller firms' growth was most evident after 1907, but the combined output of Goodyear and Firestone was still only two-thirds that of Goodrich in 1909.

Despite the growth of tire demand, the majority of the 20 or more new rubber companies established between 1904 and 1909 were general rubber goods producers rather than specialist tire firms. The most significant newcomers to automobile tire manufacture, U.S. Rubber and Michelin, each entered by taking over an existing business. The only new business to make a major impact was Firestone, and even this company's origins lay in the carriage tire trade. The Dayton Rubber Manufacturing Company added tires to its original lines of fruit jar rings and garden hose in 1910 and survived as a notable small firm until 1961. The remaining new entrants, such as Batavia Rubber and the Falls Rubber Company, were of minor importance.

On the one hand, existing tire firms' expertise provided a good basis for supplying automobile tires; this advantage may account for the limited number of new entrants. On the other hand, established skills were not completely transferable since tires, manufacturing methods, and marketing all had to be adapted. The change from bicycle and carriage to automobile tires provided the opportunity for other producers to challenge RGM's leadership. The new market undercut RGM's principal strengths. The firm's Morgan and Wright subsidiary only began automobile tire production in 1904, some eight years after Goodrich first supplied Winton.

At first U.S. automobiles were equipped with solid rubber tires, which were durable, proven on carriages, and readily available. However, the major challenge was to develop reliable pneumatic tires for automobiles. American factory managers who visited Europe emphasized the superiority of Michelin's pneumatic tires. During the early 1900s, tire makers tackled the same basic problems presented by bicycles a decade earlier, but with the extra dimensions of the automobile's greater weight and speed. Initially, manufacturers increased the size of bicycle tires, but internal friction, as the threads of fabric rubbed together, created heat, which damaged the tire. The eventual solution was to reduce the number of cross-threads, an idea taken from Palmer's cord tire patents of the 1890s. A second difficulty was the compromise between tires that stayed on the wheel rim while the vehicle was in motion and tires that could be removed easily for repair. At first the clincher principle was adopted from bicycle tires, with a hard rubber bead on the casing being squeezed inside the smaller circumference of the inturned wheel rim. This could be a tricky procedure for bicycle tires, and on the larger and heavier auto tires the clincher design required the use of a crowbar and considerable force to change a tire. It was an awkward and strenuous task and a serious matter since the early pneumatic tires often punctured and had a brief life expectancy. In response, manufacturers introduced semidetachable and fully detachable rims where, instead of being forced inside a fixed rim, the tire was placed in position and then all or part of the rim was bolted around the base of the tire using an ingenious variety of bolts and wires.

A further innovation was tread design. Automobile tires initially copied the smooth tread of bicycle tires with the result that vehicles skidded easily in wet conditions and did not always hold the road when turning sharply or at high speed. Some manufacturers fitted strips of leather or canvas around the circumference of the tire to improve its grip, but these "nonskid" covers were expensive and did not wear well. As an alternative, metal plates, wires, or rivets were vulcanized into the surface of the tread, but this "armor" tended to work loose. The eventual and far more elegant solution was the familiar patterned tread. A tread design was etched onto the inside of the vulcanizing mold and during the curing process the softened rubber tread took on the pattern. In 1908 Goodyear introduced its All-Weather tread, and Firestone, combining better traction with clever advertising, introduced an angular tread pattern that read "Firestone Non-Skid." The firm advertised that "the name prevents the slip." By 1907 manufacturers had developed sound and more durable tires, which eased the advent of the automobile age.

Since innovations were often adaptations of cycle tire developments, earlier patents retained some importance, and RGM sought to use Jeffrey's clincher patent to regulate the automobile tire business. The fate of the scheme reveals the forces changing the industry. The Clincher Tire Association was formed to license manufacturers, and the licenses stipulated annual output quotas and minimum prices. A pool commissioner received monthly sales figures from all licensees and imposed fines on firms that exceeded or fell below their quotas. In 1903 the association assigned 85 percent of the market to RGM, Goodrich, and Diamond Rubber; 7 percent to International Automobile and Vehicle Tire; and 5 percent to Fisk Rubber. Goodyear was allocated only 1.75 percent, and several new firms, including Firestone, were refused licenses. The Clincher Tire Association gave small firms a further incentive to develop alternative tire designs.

In 1900 "Nip" Scott from Cadiz, Ohio, had interested Goodyear in a machine for producing braided wire. When incorporated in the tire bead, the braided wire held the casing in place without the need for a clincher rim. Flat metal flanges, which were bolted around the rim to accommodate the tire, gave the design its name, the "straightside." By 1905 Goodyear was manufacturing 90 straightside tires daily and in the following year began licensing other firms. When the Clincher Tire Association refused Firestone a license, the company developed its own straightside tire. In 1906 Firestone undercut the Clincher Tire Association's price of $70 per set of tires in order to obtain a major contract for the new Ford Model N. This success posed a fundamental problem. Firestone could not provide national distribution of its tires to supply the potential replacement market, and its rims would not take the readily available clincher tires. Yet Ford did not want to sell a car equipped with tires that would be difficult to replace. Consequently, after a further request for a license failed, Firestone simply supplied clincher tires to Ford without approval. Ford exerted further pressure through a threat, along with other car firms outside the Association of Licensed Motor Vehicle Manufacturers, to enter tire production, and in 1906 Goodrich, well placed under the quota system, withdrew from the Clincher Tire Association. The coup de grace was administered in 1907 when a court ruled that Jeffrey's clincher patents applied only to bicycle tires.

The Firestone episode highlighted the problems caused by the variety of tire sizes and designs and emphasized the car manufacturers' interest in standard tires and rims that provided better service for the car owner. Consequently, in 1909 a majority of tire manufacturers pooled their rim patents in the United Rim Company and sought agreement on uniform specifications. Firestone remained characteristically independent and promoted its own rim designs rather than allowing other firms to use its ideas. When United Rim responded by restricting supplies to Firestone, the firm began manufacturing its own rims in 1909, the beginnings of the Firestone Steel Products Company. By 1913 and 1914 the United Rim Company was being dissolved, perhaps due to disputes between firms, such as Goodrich and U.S. Rubber, which relied on clincher rims, and Goodyear, which was promoting the straightside rim. Nevertheless, a basic standardization of tire sizes had been achieved.

Since there were few new businesses, the dramatic increase in derived demand for auto tires was met primarily by existing producers expanding output by adding workers and machinery. Employment rose swiftly. Goodrich's automobile tire department employed 940 in 1909, out of a company work force of 2,755. Diamond Rubber's total work force rose from 293 to 1,685, while Goodyear's employment increased from 51 to 522 between 1899 and 1907. Firestone's growth was more modest: 33 workers in 1904 and 103 in 1907.

During this period, manufacturing methods changed little because manufacturers concentrated on the problems of tire design. The bales of natural rubber were broken up, and the material was then washed and dried before being mixed with the vulcanizing chemicals in open mixing mills. Sheets of prepared rubber could then be pressed into cotton fabrics on calenders or used to make inner tubes, hard rubber tire beads, or heavy treads. Automobile tires were larger than bicycle tires and consequently were more difficult to assemble. The tires were built up by hand around iron, tire-shaped cores, and partly vulcanized before the heavy tread was pulled into place around the casing. The whole tire was then vulcanized in large curing ovens. A supply of skilled tire builders was, thus, vital for product quality and business success. This element may have handicapped new entrants.

Firestone's experience with the Model N contract highlighted the importance of effective distribution and stimulated a move into wholesaling. Such a strategy predated the automobile era. Goodrich opened a branch house in Chicago in 1890 and moved decisively into wholesaling from 1898; it had branches in New York, Chicago, Boston, Detroit, Buffalo, Denver, and Philadelphia within four years. Stores were also opened in Cleveland and St. Louis. In 1909 and 1910 Goodrich added six more branches and a chain of tire depots. Diamond Rubber also built up a wholesale system. The tire subsidiaries of RGM, later U.S. Rubber, had their own branches. In 1902 Goodyear bought out agencies in New York, Chicago, Boston, and St. Louis, and it established a store in Cincinnati. As automobile tire demand soared, the firm's branches increased from 5 in 1902 to 55 in 1911. Firestone began as a jobbing firm with outlets in four cities and extended its network following its entry into manufacturing, especially after the difficulties over the 1906 Ford order. Tires were both an intermediate good sold to car builders and a consumer good sold to motorists. Both aspects promoted an early move into wholesaling in order to maximize sales and to create brand loyalty. The Akron firms' swift deployment of stores increased their market penetration and presented a formidable barrier to new entrants.

☐ Akron's Emergence in the Tire Industry

As the automobile tire industry took shape, Summit County, Ohio, and especially the city of Akron, emerged as the main manufacturing center. Between 1830 and 1890 Akron's principal industries were flour milling, clay products, and farm implements. All three declined during the general depression of the 1890s, which accentuated the impact of the steady westward shift of milling and agricultural machinery production in pursuit of the farming frontier. The area still possessed such notable businesses as Quaker Oats and Diamond Match. Goodrich, the city's sole rubber company in 1889, had been joined by seven other firms by the turn of the century. By 1909 there were fourteen Akron rubber producers. Employment in the city's rubber manufacturing increased from 312 in 1889 to 2,677 at the turn of the century and totaled 19,818 by 1914. In 1909 the Akron firms sold $43.6 million worth of goods, which accounted for 33.4 percent of total "other rubber goods" sales compared with 9.3 percent in 1899.

To some extent, Akron's success was part of a broader pattern of midwestern industrialization. Ohio was one of the leading states in bicycle production, and Cincinnati specialized in the light carriages that were among the first to use rubber tires. Winton's bicycle and automobile works in Cleveland provided an important local stimulus to tire manufacture. Ohio ranked second in terms of automobile production in 1904 and 1909 as the center of the car industry shifted from Massachusetts and Connecticut to Michigan. Ohio rubber companies, therefore, had the incentive of a sizable and sustained regional demand for tires from the 1880s forward. Equally, the general acceleration of midwestern industrialization and rising real incomes made Ohio a good location for supplying a wide and expanded market for all rubber goods. The coalfields of Pennsylvania and Ohio provided the resources essential for tire production, which depended on considerable use of heat and power. Ohio was also well served by railroad links by the 1880s, which allowed the movement of natural rubber, fabrics, coal, and finished products.

The success of Akron in tire manufacturing rather than, say, Detroit, Chicago, or Cleveland reflects the influence of Goodrich. During the 1890s the firm's prosperity attracted local entrepreneurs into rubber manufacturing. Goodrich led the transition from production of bicycle and carriage tires, supplying the first U.S. pneumatic tire for a commercially produced automobile in 1896. Although not subsequently a major innovator in tire design, Goodrich was a leading firm in the early 1900s. It developed excellent manufacturing methods, established a supply of rubber to Akron, and sustained a reserve of skilled and experienced workers for the key tasks of compounding, tire building, and vulcanizing. This environment aided new ventures. The Sherbondy Rubber Company was managed by former Goodrich workers, and Firestone contracted with Goodrich for carriage tires and later for rubberized fabric. In the late 1890s Diamond Rubber's expansion further increased Akron's supply of skilled labor, which was consolidated by the formation of Goodyear, Buckeye Rubber, and Firestone.

Rubber companies in Akron were able to draw on the profits of other businesses in that city. Goodrich's initial financing by the Board of Trade was followed by investments and credit from George Crouse and later from George Perkins. Ohio Columbus Barber financed Sherbondy Rubber and Diamond Rubber out of the profits of his match company. The Seiberling family operated Akron India Rubber and then Goodyear after its earlier involvement in the milling and agricultural machinery industries as well as real estate. Frank Seiberling obtained further finance through family connections and from local businessmen, notably the Robinson and Hills families who were prominent in the local clay products industry. In the early 1900s R. C. Penfield, a relative of the Seiberlings by marriage, was Goodyear's principal backer. Harvey Firestone relied on backing from Will Christy. Such personal sources were important in the early days of all of the Akron firms, but should not be exaggerated. Frank Seiberling drew on credit from a multitude of local and midwestern banks and was an avid seller of Goodyear stock. Harvey Firestone obtained financing from the First National Bank of Chicago where he had engaged in the carriage tire trade. Buckeye Rubber was based on Consolidated Tire's profits from solid tire patents, and Goodrich developed links with New York financial markets.

On the whole, entrepreneurship was imported into Akron. Goodrich came from New York; Diamond Rubber's fastest growth followed the arrival of A. H. Marks, and Firestone had begun his business career in Chicago. The major example of local business expertise was Goodyear, which was founded and directed by Frank and Charles Seiberling. Even the Seiberlings' success depended on talented outside managers. George M. Stadelman, who became sales manager, had seven years experience with Morgan and Wright in Chicago, and Goodyear's new young factory manager, Paul W. Litchfield, was an MIT graduate who had worked briefly in eastern rubber factories.

In the early 1900s in response to demand, the principal Akron producers were able and willing to expand substantially by reinvesting profits and increasing capital. A further element in their success was effective marketing, particularly the creation of national distribution networks. Yet Akron's standing in 1909 was merely the harbinger for an even more dramatic expansion over the next decade, during which Goodrich and Diamond Rubber were challenged decisively by their previously modest neighbors, Goodyear and Firestone.

3

The Emergence of Mass Production, 1910–1916

THE TIRE INDUSTRY ENTERED A PHASE OF dynamic growth between 1910 and 1916 as production increased from 2.2 million casings to 16.9 million, doubling every two years, in response to the phenomenal expansion of motoring. On the demand side, real incomes were increasing, and the relative prosperity of the farm sector was an additional advantage for the automobile and tire industries. More significant in the timing of growth was the car manufacturers' ability to both expand output and extend their market by supplying cheaper cars. The Ford Motor Company was particularly successful in promoting lower-priced, but robust, vehicles and in applying new manufacturing and management techniques. The firm accounted for 20 percent of new car sales in 1911 and 38 percent by 1915. The other leading company was William Durant's recently assembled, though disorganized, General Motors, which supplied around 12 percent of sales in 1913. In addition there were over 200 lesser producers. There was also a much smaller, but rapidly growing, market for trucks and buses.

The burgeoning demand transformed the rubber products industry. Tires formed 19 percent of total rubber sales in 1909, but accounted for 44 percent in 1914, indicating a decisive break with the traditional prominence of footwear. Tire manufacturers increased their capacity, devised new machinery and management structures, and promoted new products. There were new entrants, but the principal challenge was by two existing firms, Goodyear and Firestone, to the two leading tire producers, Goodrich and U.S. Rubber. In the process, Akron consolidated its place as the center of the industry.

It is difficult to be precise about the structure of the tire industry in this period. Although the number of "other rubber goods" factories increased from 227 to 301 between 1909 and 1914, there were perhaps only 30 entrants to tire manufacturing. By 1915 and 1916 the rate of new company formations was accelerating with the creation of at least 23 tire firms, almost as many as in the previous seven years. The new firms tended to remain small and confined to regional markets. Such enterprises included Southern Tire and Rubber, Savage Tire, Overman Cushion Tire, and McGraw Tire and Rubber. Of more note were Gillette Rubber, Portage Rubber, and Marathon, although all three achieved their greatest significance when absorbed by major companies in the 1920s. McCreary Tire and Rubber (1915) was a tiny firm, but was to be the sole survivor into the 1980s among these smaller companies.

There were a few influential newcomers. Samson Tire and Rubber (1916) built up a good west coast trade from its Los Angeles factory. Mason Tire and Rubber (1915), based in Kent, Ohio, achieved rapid growth until the 1920s. Most important in the long term was General Tire and Rubber, established in Akron in 1915 by William O'Neil who had been a Firestone dealer in Kansas City. As Firestone progressively reduced O'Neil's district in order to create new dealerships, he formed Western Tire and Rubber in 1911 to manufacture repair materials. O'Neil then returned to Akron where his father, Michael O'Neil, owned a major department store, and in 1915 the General Tire and Rubber Company was established with capital of $200,000. William O'Neil became general manager, Michael O'Neil was company president and furnished the vital financial backing, and several Firestone managers were hired to direct the business. At first General supplied repair materials, but began tire production in 1916 and became an industry leader from the 1930s. Yet most new firms remained financially weak. They did not achieve volume production, and even the more successful newcomers had barely begun operations before 1916. The extraordinary growth in demand was, therefore, met primarily through the expansion of existing producers.

The leading producers in 1910 were U.S. Rubber, Goodrich, and Diamond Rubber. But by 1916 Goodyear and, to a lesser extent, Firestone had gained ground. U.S. Rubber's principal tire production came from the factories of Morgan and Wright, Hartford Rubber Works, and Gormully and Jeffery, and the firm accounted for perhaps 25 percent of total sales. In 1911 the U.S. Tire Company was established to coordinate marketing for the three subsidiaries, and four years later the first U.S.

Rubber trademarks were introduced in place of individual factory brands. Yet U.S. Rubber's market share had declined to 11.3 percent by 1917. In contrast, Goodrich supplied 17.6 percent of unit sales in 1909 and three years later merged with the neighboring Diamond Rubber. The new Goodrich Company, capitalized at $74 million, was the largest tire manufacturer, with a market share of between 20 and 25 percent, although its position declined thereafter. Overall these leading firms accounted for nearly 40 percent of sales in 1910 and perhaps 30 percent six years later.

Several medium-size producers each supplied 5 percent or 6 percent of sales in 1909. Fisk Rubber's market share diminished slightly, but the firm was the closest rival to the leading firms. Miller Rubber, Ajax-Grieb, Republic Rubber, Revere Rubber, and the refinanced Lee Tire and Rubber all developed as significant second-rank manufacturers. In 1912 Consolidated Rubber Tire merged its marketing operations with its production company, Buckeye Rubber, to create Kelly-Springfield. The business maintained steady growth and later moved its operations to a new plant in Maryland.

Two medium-size producers became leading firms. Goodyear's market share increased from 12 percent to 21 percent between 1910 and 1916, and the firm overtook Goodrich as the largest tire manufacturer. Firestone supplied 8 percent of sales in 1910 and 20 percent six years later, although this peak was not sustained. The success of the two firms reinforced Akron's dominant position in the industry and was the single most important response to expanding demand. Although Goodyear and Firestone gained, in part, at the expense of U.S. Rubber, the net effect of their growth and the Goodrich-Diamond Rubber merger was to increase the combined market share of the four leading firms.

An examination of individual firms' strategies and the changing nature of tire markets explains increasing industrial concentration and the successful challenge from Goodyear and Firestone. The principal influence on the industry was the extraordinary scale and speed of the growth in demand, which provided the opportunity for expansion. However, this highly favorable market provoked varied firm responses and created specific pressures that influenced the development of tire manufacturing.

By 1910 Goodyear and Firestone possessed a stronger base than other small firms. Both had made the transition into automobile tire production by stressing low prices; each was then innovative in tire design. Both had expanded rapidly after 1906 and were already large firms within the "other rubber goods" sector. Around 1909 Goodyear employed 1,820 workers and Firestone's work force had mushroomed to

1,000 compared with the "other rubber goods" industry average of 116 workers. Despite such solid credentials, both firms were far smaller than Goodrich. Goodyear and Firestone relied on internal growth and specialized more in tires than either Goodrich or U.S. Rubber. Such specialization was advantageous in that resources were concentrated on the most dynamic sector of the rubber industry.

The decisive factor in the subsequent expansion of Goodyear and Firestone was the OE market, which accounted for 29 percent of unit tire sales between 1910 and 1917. The market provided large orders as well as the prospect of future replacement purchases. Car firms obtained quotations from several producers and were able to hold down OE tire prices; in 1914 OE prices were around 80 percent of wholesale tire prices. During the early 1900s the major car firms, such as Winton and Packard, produced expensive vehicles, and their business was handled principally by Goodrich, U.S. Rubber, and Diamond Rubber. Goodyear had some success in obtaining contracts with Oakland, Cadillac, Overland, and Ford, while Michelin sold to Buick and Reo. Firestone's major breakthrough was the Ford Model N contract in 1906.

Between 1908 and 1917 the automobile industry was altered fundamentally by the shift toward volume production of cheaper cars. In the process Ford and General Motors superseded Winton, Packard, Locomobile, Pierce-Arrow, and the other makers of luxury models. There was pressure for lower prices, and Goodyear and Firestone were well placed, through their established contacts with the producers of low- and medium-priced cars, to obtain a major share of the expanding market. Between 1908 and 1912 Goodyear's OE sales increased from 12,736 to 482,784 tires, and in 1916 the firm accounted for 32 percent of the OE market. Goodyear's contracts included Buick, Chevrolet, and Ford, and OE business provided over half of the company's tire sales. Goodyear president, Frank Seiberling, cultivated a close relationship with GM's Durant, while the firm's sales manager, George Stadelman, directed an aggressive OE sales campaign. Firestone developed close links with the Ford Motor Company.

Goodrich, Diamond Rubber, and U.S. Rubber were by no means excluded from the OE market because automobile producers preferred to use several firms, both to maintain low prices and ensure good supplies. Nonetheless, the emergence of Ford and General Motors accelerated the growth of Goodyear and Firestone, enabling them to challenge the industry leaders. Small producers and new entrants were rarely able to compete with the established contracts and low prices of OE suppliers. Thus, the sector became the province of large firms. The extent of participation in the OE business was related directly to firm size by

1915. Few OE suppliers and the explosive growth in automobile output created barriers to later entrants.

Price was the single most important element for OE contracts, particularly with Ford, but distribution, tire quality, and credit arrangements were also significant. OE demand fluctuated seasonally, and volume orders required tire firms to incur significant inventory costs and be willing to provide easy terms to car firms. The latter could create financial uncertainty, especially as rubber prices, the major cost, were volatile. Between 1900 and 1910 the limitations of rubber supply and rapidly increasing consumption produced wide price swings. A phase of declining rubber prices to 1908 was followed by an increase from 82 cents per pound to $1.91 between 1908 and 1910. Manufacturers could benefit from windfall profits on rubber purchases, but had to be cautious in taking on long-term orders. When Buick delayed payments to Goodyear at the peak of rubber prices, the tire firm had to sustain large financial commitments through bank borrowing. Such financial support was essential to retain OE contracts. Even after the entrance of southeast Asian plantations into the market drove down rubber prices between 1910 and 1915, price competition in the OE market persisted because the producers undercut their rivals in anticipation of declining costs.

Replacement tires accounted for 69 percent of total output in 1915 and were divided between commercial account sales to large consumers, such as taxi firms, and retail sales to the general public. Commercial account tires sold at around 85 percent of list price, rather more than OE prices, while individual consumers paid list unless dealers offered discounts. Private motorists provided the largest and most profitable market. Manufacturers handled commercial account sales directly from the factory, and sales managers varied their prices depending on the size of each order. During the early 1900s replacement tires were supplied through independent wholesalers and retailers, and all tire dealers carried many different brands. The leading manufacturers, however, soon moved into wholesaling and this process of vertical integration accelerated as sales increased across the United States.

Car manufacturers favored suppliers who could ensure effective national distribution, and low OE prices and profit margins were based on the assumption, even necessity, of subsequent replacement orders. Consequently, the leading firms built national systems of branch houses. A branch store allowed more control over discounting policies and, potentially, a more consistent financial return on sales. There was a greater risk from larger inventories of finished tires whose value was vulnerable to price changes, but such inventory costs simply gave clearer and formal recognition to the existing and diverse credit arrangements with wholesalers and retailers.

Goodrich's early wholesale stores were for its general rubber business, but a chain of tire depots was formed in 1910 to supply the scattered replacement market. Diamond Rubber had some forty branch stores by 1912 when the firm merged with Goodrich, but the new firm pruned its branch network. Goodyear performed all of its own wholesaling by 1912, thereby giving maximum promotion to its own brands. Firestone, Fisk, and U.S. Rubber pursued the same strategy. Fisk possessed 90 branch stores by 1915, which handled 80 percent of company sales, with the remainder accounted for by OE orders. By 1914 Firestone had 23 branches, several controlled through regional subsidiaries, as well as over 100 service stations supplying and fitting truck tires. U.S. Rubber's subsidiaries operated their own wholesale outlets until 1911, when the branches and sales departments were placed under the control of the newly formed U.S. Tire Company. U.S. Tire's eastern, central, and Pacific sales districts supplied over 4,000 distributors. A few small firms did enter wholesaling, but generally lagged far behind the leading firms. The extent of national distribution was a further element separating large and small producers as early as 1909.

As central sales departments and sales forces expanded, manufacturers developed their relationship with retailers through dealer programs. Branch houses ceased all retail sales and allocated territories to dealers according to the size of local markets. Firms provided advertising material, marketing advice, and additional discounts for prompt payment or advance orders. Occasionally manufacturers made concerted efforts to enforce retail price lists and to reduce discounts in cases of price cutting. Yet such steps toward more formal relationships were faltering because the desire for rapid growth militated against strict control, especially since firms often could not meet their dealers' demands. Dealers complained about reductions in their territories and "indiscriminate" selection of new outlets; some changed suppliers frequently. Moreover dealerships varied in size, location, expenses, and sales policy. In the generally buoyant retail market, producers had little effective sanction over dealers' prices.

After the collapse of the clincher pool, manufacturers may have set prices with reference to Goodrich's list price; Ralph and Howard Wolf refer to a "gentleman's agreement" between Goodrich and Diamond before 1912 (Wolf and Wolf, *Rubber*, 427–28). In 1909 and 1911 the two firms notified the trade about impending price reductions, which Goodyear followed. Such uniformity, however, was strictly limited.

Manufacturers and dealers offered a variety of discounts, which were encouraged by declining rubber prices after 1910 and by efforts to recoup business following a rubber workers' strike in Akron in 1913. The increasing market shares of Goodyear and Firestone further undermined any price accord. In early 1914 Goodrich and Goodyear discussed the issue of pricing policy, but they hesitated over legal considerations and then engaged in intense OE competition. By October 1914, Goodrich's president, H. E. Raymond, angrily proclaimed that there "never has and never will be any agreement between our companies that restricts freedom in making prices" (H. E. Raymond to F. A. Seiberling, 19 October 1914, F. A. Seiberling Papers, coll. 347, Ohio Historical Society).

The lack of agreement on prices largely reflected the nature of tire markets, particularly the bargaining power of the major car manufacturers. It was also, however, one manifestation of an independent streak that characterized many entrepreneurs in the tire business. Goodyear and Firestone established their positions by challenging patent restrictions where such arrangements did not serve their interests. Harvey Firestone's success and tight control over his firm enabled him to pursue a lone course over patents, prices, and industry policy into the 1930s. Frank Seiberling was in a similar position at Goodyear until 1920. Even in the 1920s Paul Litchfield was sufficiently dominant to determine the direction of Goodyear's policy. Family control also existed at General Tire and among many smaller companies.

As demand boomed, the leading producers' success depended on expanded output through new investment. The Morgan and Wright plant in Detroit increased its capacity by 20 percent in 1909, and Gormully and Jeffrey's plant capacity doubled. Goodrich's daily capacity increased from 1,050 tires in 1909 to 8,500 in 1914 following the merger with Diamond; it was estimated at 20,000 tires in 1916. Goodyear's daily capacity grew from 600 tires in 1909, to 4,000 in 1913, over 10,000 by 1915, and 15,000 tires a year later. Firestone's daily capacity rose to around 15,000 over the same period. Such rapid growth required further expansion in employment and new investment, plus technical change.

Goodyear's factory workforce increased from 1,815 to 12,318 between 1906 and 1916, with 80 percent working in tire production. Firestone employed 1,000 workers in 1909 and 7,100 in 1916. In Akron the rapid growth began with the introduction of night shifts around 1907, and the larger manufacturers adopted a system of three eight-hour shifts after 1912. In common with other manufacturing industries labor turnover was high, especially in Akron where many firms competed for labor. Workers moved in response to even minor wage differentials. Consequently, the Akron firms recruited widely, and the industry's overall growth was reflected in the city's population, which rose from 69,027 to 100,079 between 1910 and 1915.

All firms made frequent and substantial additions to their factories. Many companies, notably Firestone in 1911, opened imposing new multistory plants with improved layouts. Since demand continually pressed on capacity, factories soon became congested and inadequate. Consequently, technical change was important, especially as the shift toward cheaper automobiles exerted pressure for lower tire prices. Since tire sizes had been standardized, the environment was favorable for innovation, and in contrast to the previous decade, there were numerous important developments in manufacturing technology. Between 1909 and 1919 output per man-hour in rubber manufacturing increased at an annual average rate of 7.8 percent, faster than any other manufacturing industry. The rubber industry's productivity growth was concentrated in tire manufacture and reflected a mix of mechanical, chemical, and organizational innovations.

An established trend towards improving standard equipment gathered momentum, and the capacity of mixing mills and calenders increased. From 1912 direct drives from electric motors and improved gears and clutches permitted faster and more controlled machine speeds, and electrification proceeded rapidly. The preparation of natural rubber also changed. During the early 1900s wild rubber required careful washing and then was hung in sheets for several days to dry. The switch to plantation rubber around 1910 provided a cleaner and more homogeneous raw material requiring less preparation. Moreover, the adoption of vacuum drying between 1909 and 1912 cut drying times to a few hours, thereby reducing inventory costs. With plantation rubbers, larger batches could be mixed with greater certainty of producing a standard compound that was easier to handle without scorching or partly vulcanizing during the manufacturing process.

The companies' research laboratories also contributed to advances in rubber chemistry, notably the wider and more sophisticated use of chemicals that accelerated vulcanization or allowed differential rates of vulcanization for each part of the casing. Previously, casings had been cured once before the tread was fitted and then a second time with the tread in place. Otherwise, the thick tread prevented complete vulcanization of the inner layers of the casing. Accelerators, however, permitted a single cure with significant economies in the use of heat and the time involved in vulcanization. The pace of innovation varied considerably. George Oenslager pioneered the development of accelerators at Diamond Rubber from 1906, but Goodyear, for example, did not adopt the single cure until 1918.

The most obvious innovation was the use of carbon black rather than zinc oxide as a strengthening agent. Diamond pioneered the new material in 1912, and the effect was to color tires black instead of their original gray-white.

The most important innovation was the partial mechanization of casing assembly with the development of the core tire-building machine. Before 1909 each casing was constructed by hand around an iron core shaped like an inner tube. Tire builders fitted each ply around the core individually, spreading rubber cement between the plies, and stitching each one down. Considerable strength and dexterity was required to pull the plies around the core and hold them in place. It was a highly skilled job because any wrinkles or air bubbles produced distortions in the final casing. Each casing contained two beads, one around each side of the base, which were placed between the first and second plies, and cushion and breaker strips were included for extra strength. After the first vulcanization there was the arduous task of fitting the heavy rubber tread in place to complete the casing. Given its complexity, difficulty, and fundamental effect on tire quality, tire building was a strategically important operation in any expansion of output.

During the 1890s and early 1900s several tire-building machines were patented for solid and pneumatic tires. These were technically unsatisfactory, and the hand process was better suited to the numerous tire sizes. Moreover, the industry concentrated on tire design and quality rather than production. By 1908, however, reliable pneumatic tires were available, and the priority was increased output so tire production received new attention. Goodyear, Goodrich, and Diamond acquired Vincent tire-building machines from France, but these proved inferior to the hand process. Nonetheless, John Gammeter of Goodrich devised a machine based on the imported technology, and Goodyear's chief engineer, W. C. State, patented a new design in 1909. By August 1909 Goodrich had thirty machines in use, and Goodyear possessed six. The machines retained the iron core of the hand process, but applied electrical power to rotate the core. A turret above the core held the tire builder's tools: stitching rollers, spinning rollers, a bead attaching roller, and tread roller. The different rollers maintained an even tension on the tire and, thus, reduced the strength involved in assembling the casing. The tire builder's skill and dexterity remained decisive, but the machines simplified the task. Overall, core machines increased a tire builder's daily output from 6 or 8 casings to between 20 and 40 depending on tire size. There were also savings on floor space and an improvement in the uniformity and, thus, durability of the finished product.

Goodrich continued to rely on machines supplied by its own workshops, but Goodyear's State patent became the mechanism for wider diffusion of the technology. The firm licensed other manufacturers and supplied State machines in return for royalties on each tire produced subject to a guaranteed minimum payment. Morgan and Wright, Gormully and Jeffrey, Hartford Rubber Works, Revere Rubber, and Fisk had all obtained licenses by 1910 and were followed by several smaller firms. The involvement of U.S. Rubber's plants ensured that the State patent was profitable: royalty income increased from $43,767 in 1910 to $355,428 in 1916.

Many small producers preferred cheaper machines supplied by engineering companies, notably three Trenton firms: J. E. Thropp, W. R. Thropp, and Delaski-Thropp. By 1914 25 producers were using the various Thropp machines. This competition reduced the cost of machines and State's royalty charges. Goodyear initiated litigation in 1914 against Thropp and Firestone, alleging infringement of the State patent. Firestone had initially refused to seek a State license and instead relied on hand construction despite its increasing inefficiency. In 1912, however, Firestone hired W. C. Stevens, an engineer who had experimented previously on core machines at both Goodyear and Goodrich, and within a year Stevens had brought 20 machines into operation in the Firestone plant. The patent suits proved long and tortuous: a district court found in Goodyear's favor, then the Appeal Court reversed the decision, and finally its dismissal of Goodyear's claims was confirmed by the U.S. Supreme Court in 1923. In the interim core tire building was adopted widely and was a major element in the industry's ability to expand output and raise productivity. The core process was superseded gradually in the 1920s by a new "drum" method of tire building.

The introduction of tire-building machines led to a six-week strike in Akron during 1913, the industry's most significant labor dispute before 1935. The underlying cause of the strike was the tire firms' increased emphasis on time-study methods to set piece rates. Between 1909 and 1912 the number of tire builders in Akron increased from 1,333 to 3,888 or from around 10 percent to 20 percent of the work force. The core machines permitted increased output, and tire builders enjoyed higher earnings until rates were reduced. Tire builders responded by establishing an informal, but effective, "soldiering" agreement based on producing enough to earn around $3.50 a day. In 1912 Goodyear removed all limits on piece-rate earnings to encourage greater output, and the soldiering system collapsed as some tire builders earned up to $4.75 a day. The firm conducted time studies and finally issued a revised piece-rate schedule for machine tire building. The workers alleged that Goodyear was enforcing a speedup and reducing earnings; management claimed the lower rates allowed a fair wage without undue effort. In February 1913 a similar sequence of events occurred in Firestone's factory following the introduction of Stevens's tire-building machines. Firestone tire finishers walked out, and within days two-thirds of the Akron industry was on strike. Workers complained about wage rates, speedup, time studies, and factory conditions, while employers blamed the strike on the Industrial Workers of the World, a radical labor union then at its peak. An Ohio Senate committee was appointed to investigate the dispute. Its final report endorsed managerial evidence of improved conditions, but the strike had already collapsed in the face of financial weakness and orchestrated community opposition. The dispute strengthened managerial control but also ensured that the continuing expansion of the workforce was accompanied by the extension of formal employment conditions, new management systems to check arbitrary actions by foremen and employee welfare schemes.

The 1913 strike indicated the changing character of tire manufacturing in the face of expanding demand. The management structures of firms were changing. On the one hand, managers tried to maximize output through technical changes and to improve efficiency in all aspects of their factory operations. This approach was reflected in the increased application of time-study methods in setting piece rates and the appearance of managers with special responsibility for such matters. The creation of Goodyear's Efficiency Department in 1915 was evidence of the new style of factory management. Yet such departments were hard pressed as the sheer scale of growth continually disrupted plans and posed new challenges.

On the other hand, managers sought to devise organizations that could cope with their rapidly expanding workforces. The major Akron firms, particularly Goodyear and Firestone, led the way in such innovations in labor relations. The Akron firms encountered difficulties in retaining labor, especially skilled workers, given the number of competing firms, varying wage rates, and the arduous nature of the work. In response the major firms continued to develop more formal employment conditions and transferred authority over hiring and firing from foremen to labor and personnel departments.

Goodyear's personnel program was particularly extensive. A relief association was established in 1909, a factory magazine, restaurant, and hospital were added in 1912, paid vacations in 1914, and insurance and pensions schemes during 1915–16. Firestone's new Industrial Service

Department took responsibility for factory safety in 1913; the firm opened a club house in 1916 with extensive sports facilities and introduced medical services, insurance, a savings bank, and employee stock ownership. Goodrich provided pension and insurance plans, and many smaller firms had at least rudimentary medical facilities. The city's growth strained local housing and social services. Both Goodyear and Firestone promoted housing developments: Goodyear Heights and Seiberling Field in 1912 and Firestone Park after 1916.

4

Growth and Instability, 1916–1921

BETWEEN 1916 AND 1921 THE EXTRAORDI-
nary expansion of tire output continued, but the industry met the first
real obstacles linked to the brief impact of war and the more profound
effect of the 1920–21 recession. Automobile production trebled between
1914 and 1919 with the only interruption coming in 1918 when the
government restricted civilian car output. Registrations grew even more
rapidly than vehicle production after 1914. Although the rates of
growth slackened compared to the early 1900s, the volume of automobile output and use rose substantially until the postwar recession curtailed new car sales. The trends in tire sales are summarized in Table
4.1. The impact of wartime controls and the postwar recession are
evident in fluctuating OE sales. The growth of replacement business
remained extremely rapid to 1918, but was also checked in 1921.

The outbreak of war in Europe in 1914 disrupted the natural rubber
trade, but American manufacturers were able to bypass European rubber markets as well as increasing their consumption of recycled rubber.
Despite periods of volatility, average rubber prices increased only in
1916 and remained below prewar levels. The war curtailed European
competition in export markets, leaving U.S. manufacturers well placed
to exploit their ability to maintain supplies and output. It was a significant stage in the development of the overseas activities of U.S. firms
because new markets were extended and later defended. Nonetheless,
exports accounted for less than 4 percent of American tire sales. The

Table 4.1. Unit Sales of Automobile Tires, 1914–21

	OE	Replacement	Total	Index of Total Sales (1914=100)
1914	2,175,000	6,008,000	8,183,000	100
1916	6,139,000	10,782,000	16,921,000	207
1918	4,046,000	20,494,000	24,540,000	300
1920	8,472,000	20,565,000	29,037,000	355
1921	6,299,000	21,973,000	28,272,000	345

Source: Gaffey, *The Productivity of Labor in the Rubber Tire Manufacturing Industry*, 54, Table 6. Copyright 1940 by Columbia University Press. Used by permission.

domestic market remained paramount and was barely affected by the war before 1917, except that wartime farm prosperity strengthened rural demand for automobiles.

During 1917, tire production increased by 40 percent, primarily because of replacement demand. There were several new market entrants, but only Carlisle Tire and Rubber developed to any degree. The recently formed General Tire launched an advertising campaign, extended its dealerships, and added to its plant after the firm established itself in the high-price end of the market. Dayton Rubber strengthened its tire division by opening a new factory. The leading firms increased capacity, and despite the overall diversity of tires, they placed greater emphasis on volume production of the most popular sizes. Goodyear opened a new plant in Akron in 1916 that concentrated on the manufacture of the firm's best-selling tires, while Firestone's second factory, which began operations in 1917, was devoted to tires for Ford's Model T. New investment and the continuing move to eight-hour shifts contributed to further rapid growth in employment. Goodyear employed 5,820 workers in 1915, rising to 16,875 in 1916; Firestone's workforce doubled from 5,000 in 1915 to 10,500 in 1917.

Following U.S. entry into the war in April 1917, mechanical goods, footwear, clothing, and rubber cement were required in greater quantities as well as new specialized equipment such as gas masks, fuel tanks, and observation balloons. Firestone's new tire plant was converted to balloon production, and Goodyear's balloon room employed 2,800 workers by 1918. Both Goodyear and Goodrich expanded their manufacture of nonrigid airships, and the expansion of aircraft production provided a new market for tires able to cope with the demands of advancing aircraft technology.

The largest new element was the demand for solid tires for military and commercial vehicles. Firestone was the major supplier, reflecting its origins as a solid tire business. Goodyear was a close second. Goodrich, U.S. Rubber, and smaller producers, such as Fisk, Swinehart, Kelly-Springfield, and Republic, also increased their production of solid tires. Firms accelerated their experimental work on pneumatic truck tires, which, though providing only a small fraction of wartime needs, were to supersede solid tires by the late 1920s.

Overall, military demand promoted greater diversification by Goodyear and Firestone, the tire specialists, and temporarily strengthened Goodrich's mechanical goods department and U.S. Rubber's mechanical, chemical, and footwear divisions. The existing pressures on capacity and labor supplies intensified since manufacturers increased output while losing male workers to the armed forces. The recruitment of women workers, particularly in balloon and gas mask production, provided additional labor, but the persistent scarcity of workers was reflected in rapidly increasing wages. Civilian tire supplies were maintained at the outset of 1917 because firms had accumulated reserves of rubber and were increasing production capacity. The first indication of the war's impact was the leading firms' inability to meet their dealers' demands in full. Goodyear advised some dealers to purchase other tire brands in 1917.

The degree of mobilization and regulation increased substantially in 1918. The War Trade Board restricted rubber imports, established prices, and allocated supplies for military priorities. The Akron industry received less than half of its normal rubber supply in 1918, fuel was rationed, and federal conservation policies included standardization of tire sizes and the discontinuation of some products. Manufacturers placed greater emphasis on obtaining military contracts for which additional raw materials were released, and this strategy was given added impetus when the War Industries Board restricted automobile output to 50 percent of its 1917 level to conserve steel. The resulting fall in OE sales during 1918 compelled major tire producers to rely increasingly on the growth of solid tire and nontire business. Total tire sales increased slightly in 1918 due to the continued growth of replacement demand, and small firms may have benefited from the leading manufacturers' inability to supply all dealers.

The brief phase of war production ended swiftly. Controls on rubber supplies were removed in December 1918, the automobile industry resumed full civilian production, and OE sales increased from 4 million to 7.2 million casings between 1918 and 1919. Goodyear captured 49 percent of the OE market in 1919 compared with 32 percent in 1916, and Firestone was also well placed. By contrast, U.S. Rubber and Goodrich found their prewar OE market shares difficult to regain. Replacement sales expanded further to 30.6 million casings in 1919. During 1919 at least 44 new ventures were started, a record number of new entrants, which reflected postwar optimism. The newcomers were virtually all minor producers and included some financial promotions that never manufactured tires. The only notable businesses were McClaren, which was absorbed by Dayton Rubber in 1935, and Grand Rapids Tire and Rubber, which later became Corduroy. Steady growth remained the province of established producers.

With automobile companies forecasting greater sales, prospects again appeared favorable in 1920. The tire industry planned for expansion. Goodrich initiated a $10 million construction program, and Firestone's authorized capital was raised from $15 million to $75 million to provide working capital and to finance new capacity. Goodyear opened a factory in Los Angeles to supply the western states. U.S. Rubber planned to double capacity through a major expansion of its five tire plants. Babcock estimated that the industry's capital investment totaled $105 million in 1920, a level not surpassed in the interwar years. All firms reported labor shortages due to high rates of turnover. Against this background, manufacturers accumulated larger stocks of tires and entered into longer-term contracts for fabrics, rubber, and cotton to ensure stable supplies. Major OE suppliers were particularly committed: Firestone signed three-year contracts for raw materials, and Goodyear had on hand six months' supply of rubber, valued at $20 million above its actual cost, by early 1920.

The predicted expansion began in October 1919, and by April 1920 sales were more than 50 percent above 1918–19 levels. Thereafter, demand slackened in the economic recession between January 1920 and July 1921. Automobile manufacturers canceled orders and postponed payments during the sales slump. Despite an overall increase of 17 percent in OE sales during 1920, demand did not reach the anticipated levels, leaving the leading producers with sizable inventories of materials and tires.

Raw material prices moved down sharply in the general deflation of 1920–21. In common with most other sectors, the industry's borrowing and commitments in 1919 for expansion now represented a serious financial burden. Moreover, there was no respite in the replacement market where sales declined by 12 percent, showing for the first time that consumers could postpone tire purchases. Smaller firms depended on replacement sales, and the swift contraction in demand exposed their financial weakness. Desperate price cutting occurred by mid-1920 as firms sought cash and lower inventories. All firms reduced employment, wages, and salaries, placed more workers on piece rates, halted new investment, and postponed or canceled raw material orders.

In August 1920, Harvey Firestone returned hurriedly from a European vacation as his company's debt reached $43.9 million. He assumed personal control of the sales department, lambasted his own organization for excessive bureaucracy, and sanctioned a sales campaign in October 1920 based on price reductions of 25 percent. Between May and November 1920, Firestone's factory work force was reduced from 13,755 to 3,215. Firestone was one of the few firms to record an upturn in unit sales during the year, and by December the company's debt had declined to $31.3 million. Common stock dividends were paid to January 1921, but then passed until the firm's debts were finally cleared in 1924. Preferred dividends continued throughout. Firestone's strategy accelerated the trend toward price cutting; Goodrich, Mason, and Miller initiated further discounting in December 1920.

The new year proved equally difficult. OE demand fell from 8.4 million to 6.2 million tires, exacerbating the problems of Goodyear and Firestone. Replacement sales recovered in the spring, increasing overall from 20.5 million tires in 1920 to 21.9 million in 1921, which resulted in a slight increase in overall tire output. Yet the industry required only 60 percent of its capacity, prices remained low, and discounting was widespread so that earnings were poor. Goodrich triggered further price competition in May 1921. The fundamental problems created by surplus capacity and debt were given an added twist by declining raw material prices, which contributed to the leading manufacturers' massive losses on inventories and forward contracts. Despite relative caution in 1919, U.S. Rubber had to write down its raw material inventories by $11.1 million and finished goods by $6.1 million. Medium-size producers also suffered: the value of Miller Rubber's inventories fell by $3.4 million. Since the length of raw material commitments was directly related to firm size, smaller companies were most rapidly able to buy at current price levels. Thus, during 1921 major firms were disadvantaged, while surviving small and medium-size producers were temporarily better placed to maintain low prices. Competition remained intense even when demand began to recover, and since nontire sales were also poor, there was no relief from other rubber markets.

In this environment Goodyear, the industry's largest and most dynamic firm, came close to bankruptcy, and Frank and Charles Seiberling lost control of the business. Goodyear's crisis reflected both general conditions and the firm's particular position and management strategy. During 1917 and 1918 Goodyear's large raw material reserves led to delays in paying bills and suggestions from bankers that the firm was overextended. Frank Seiberling was conscious of the dangers of a postwar deflation, although he regarded bankers as unduly conservative. Yet the transition to civilian production proved reasonably smooth, and Goodyear's inventories increased once more. The episode convinced Seiberling to reduce dependence on bank lending by selling company stock. Goodyear's authorized capital was raised from $20 million in 1917 to $200 million in 1919, although issued capital rose far more modestly from $44.6 million to $57.4 million. Past profits and current demand justified expansion, but there was pressure to maintain dividends to promote sales of stock. Goodyear's lack of strong links with the financial sector became a weakness in 1920.

During 1919 Goodyear manufactured 7.5 million tires, an extraordinary 97 percent of capacity, and the sales department still emphasized its inability to meet demand. The firm captured half of the OE market and, therefore, amassed major raw material commitments. As a result of this success, Goodyear was particularly exposed to the contraction of automobile sales in 1920 and to the collapse of rubber and cotton prices. The first sign of concern over inventories was a reduction of monthly output in Akron from 800,000 tires in March to 100,000 tires by December 1920, with capacity utilization in 1920 falling to only 64 percent. The value of sales remained high until May 1920, but then slumped from $20.4 million to $4.6 million by the end of the year. OE orders were canceled, and Ford, also seeking to conserve cash, paid in company notes. Goodyear raised $27.8 million from its shareholders by new issues and added new tire dealers in a bid to improve sales. The sales organization was also used to sell shares to employees, dealers, and the public. As creditors pressed for payment, the firm obtained temporary loans in November 1920, but this merely delayed the final crisis. In January 1921 management, bankers, and creditors met to discuss the company's future. Outstanding debts to banks and suppliers totaled $65.9 million, and there was a further $55 million of commitments for future deliveries of tire fabrics and other materials. In an extraordinary transformation, the postwar recession had left the leading tire producer facing the possibility of bankruptcy.

Goodyear's creditors preferred the option of a reorganization. Four committees were established representing bank creditors, merchandise creditors, preferred stockholders, and common stockholders. The refinancing was organized by Dillon, Read, New York investment bankers with a Chicago office. The scheme provided some $90 million in new securities, all owners of which were guaranteed prior preference over existing shareholders as well as the right to elect a majority of the company's directors. There were three key elements in the refinancing. Dillon, Read took $30 million in twenty-year bonds, which paid 8 percent interest and were issued at 90 percent of par and callable at 120 percent. Second, the bank creditors' and the merchandise creditors' committees agreed to distribute the remaining new securities. There was $27.5 million in ten-year debentures with an 8 percent interest rate, issued at 90 and callable at 110 percent of par; each debenture was accompanied by one share of common stock. A further $33 million was raised in prior preference stock. The third element was $10,000 in management stock, which provided control over a majority of seats on the board. Clarence Dillon, John Sherwin of Union Trust, and Owen Young of General Electric were appointed as trustees of the management stock, representing Dillon, Read, bank creditors, and merchandise creditors, respectively. As late as March 1921, Frank A. Seiberling appeared hopeful of remaining on the board, but in May he and brother Charles resigned at the first meeting following the refinancing. George Stadelman and Paul Litchfield remained directors and in control of sales and production, but E. G. Wilmer, a businessman with links to Dillon, Read, became president. A five-year management contract was signed with Leonard Kennedy and Company, also linked to Dillon, Read, and 27 new executives were appointed to undertake a reorganization.

The first act was a scathing assessment of Goodyear's organization, particularly the accounting, budgetary, legal, and purchasing departments. Wilmer reported that indebtedness had been underestimated because there was no clear record of orders for fabrics, rubber, or cotton, and no effective control over expenditure. The firm's dealers were alleged to be unreliable. The new management claimed that the factories contained obsolete machinery and too many foremen. The overall picture was a lax and fragmented organization, lacking central direction. The criticisms were not entirely disinterested, but demoralization and chaos had undoubtedly resulted from Goodyear's recent contraction: factory employment had declined from 31,421 to 6,363 and the office staff from 1,604 to 642 in the year ending May 1921.

The firm's position was far from unique. The recession prompted very similar assessments at Firestone, Ford Motor Company, General Motors, and many other large corporations that had expanded rapidly since the turn of the century. Despite the creation of management structures, the pronounced swings in output, employment, and prices during and immediately after the war had been destabilizing. Equally, Frank Seiberling's entrepreneurial approach had emphasized expansion at all costs with rather precarious financial direction. His confident style had brought Goodyear's phenomenal growth. The recession made such imprecise accounting a liability for the first time since 1904. Yet, while inadequate financing was the immediate cause of the crisis, Wilmer's criticisms of both sales and production raised questions about the management qualities of Stadelman and Litchfield who both survived the reorganization to become company presidents during the 1920s.

Despite tighter financial control, Goodyear struggled throughout 1921. The firm's Akron plants operated at only 42 percent of capacity compared with an industry average of 60 percent, and its OE market share declined from 39 percent to 28 percent in 1921 as other firms bid aggressively for orders. While Goodyear remained the largest tire producer, its total market share had fallen from 25 percent in 1919 to 16 percent by 1921. At the same time the dramatic changes in employment and the labor market were reflected in a substantial decline in labor turnover and a 79 percent increase in labor productivity. Both situations were maintained during the 1920s as new labor-saving technology promoted productivity and reduced the proportion of unskilled labor among whom turnover had been particularly high.

Goodyear's revival began in 1922, when output expanded to 7.1 million tires and sales increased from $112.5 million to $175.5 million as the economy picked up. Although Goodyear used only 63 percent of its capacity, the firm had finally absorbed its high-price fabric. Moreover, a shift from fabric to cord tires, especially in a resurgent OE market, benefited Goodyear, which had concentrated on developing the new product.

Although essential, the 1921 refinancing increased Goodyear's capitalization substantially, and as interest rates fell, the 8 percent interest on the bonds and debentures was a high cost. Repayment was made more difficult by continuing price competition and generally lower earnings. Between 1921 and 1926 the prior preference commitments were reduced by over $35 million, but $54.7 million remained outstanding. One effect was to restrict Goodyear's working capital, especially when rubber prices were very high in 1925. Preferred and common stockholders resented their lack of dividends, and Frank Seiberling persistently criticized the 1921 refinancing and Dillon, Read's influence.

In 1923 a shareholder's suit led to the termination of Leonard Kennedy and Company's management contract, and there were several attempts to devise a refinancing acceptable to the various interests. Finally in 1926, Litchfield, the company's new president, proposed new bond and stock issues to redeem the 1921 debt. At the same time, common and preferred stockholders' committees began litigation seeking to remove Clarence Dillon and John Sherwin as trustees of the management stock and demanding a full accounting of Goodyear's finances since 1921. A countersuit charged Frank Seiberling with improper use of company funds before 1921. A refinancing was finally agreed upon in June 1927, despite continuing opposition, and the 1921 prior preference securities were redeemed, including the management stock. Dividend payments resumed, at perhaps unduly high levels, in 1929 and 1930. The settlement in 1927 consolidated Litchfield's control over policy and provided more working capital; both factors contributed to a significantly more expansionary and aggressive strategy.

The 1920–21 recession affected the tire industry fundamentally. The short-term effect was to weaken Goodyear and, to a lesser extent, other major firms, while many new enterprises failed either immediately or more slowly via reorganizations or mergers. Surviving small firms took temporary advantage of low raw material prices to compete effectively in the early 1920s with larger firms still working off expensive inventories. The trend toward rising concentration was checked briefly. More generally, the experience of 1920–21 increased financial influence over policy and ensured a more conservative approach to raw material orders and inventories. The resulting preference for larger rubber reserves in case of price fluctuations contributed to significantly lower levels of profits and dividends during the 1920s. In hindsight the recession also signaled a degree of maturity for the automobile and tire industries. Despite substantial increases in output after 1921, the number of firms and new entrants declined, as did profit levels, and the industry entered a highly competitive era.

5

Concentration and Competition in the 1920s

THE UNCERTAINTIES OF THE 1920–21 RE-
cession foreshadowed two decades of change and difficulty in the tire
industry. Table 5.1 shows the number of factories, employment, and
output between the wars. Despite the recession, there were 178 factories
in 1921 and over 160 separate firms, employing 55,496 workers and
producing 30.4 million tires. During the 1920s, output more than doubled and employment revived, yet without regaining the peak of 1919.
The number of manufacturers declined to 62 firms in 1929 compared
with 166 in 1923, a reduction of almost two-thirds. The 1930s depression continued the attrition, leaving 35 companies in 1933. There was a
marked increase in average size of plant between 1921 and 1929 and
further significant increases in the 1930s, which indicate that smaller
firms bore the brunt of the contraction.

In 1921 the industry was dominated by five large companies:
Goodyear, Goodrich, Firestone, U.S. Rubber, and Fisk. Below this level
were several medium-size firms, notably Kelly-Springfield, Miller Rubber, Mansfield, and the expanding General Tire. Further down the scale
was a third rank of about a dozen small, but still significant, producers,
such as Mason, Gates, Dayton, Pharis, the American plants of Michelin
and Dunlop, and the newly formed Seiberling Rubber. The remainder of
the industry consisted of over one hundred tiny firms, including
McCreary, Armstrong, Lake Shore Tire and Rubber, and Carolina Rubber Company. Table 5.2 shows the changing industrial structure using

Table 5.1. Factories, Employment, and Output in Tire Manufacturing,
1921–37

				Indices of Average Plant Size (1921 = 100)	
Year	Factories	Employment	Tire Output (thousands)	Average Employment	Average Tire Output
1921	178	55,496	30,490	100	100
1923	160	73,963	43,977	148	160
1925	126	81,640	57,656	208	267
1927	109	78,256	61,600	230	330
1929	91	83,263	66,474	293	426
1931	48	49,159	48,412	328	589
1933	44	52,976	45,376	386	602
1935	42	57,128	48,765	436	678
1937	46	63,290	54,113	441	687

Source: French, "Structural Change and Competition in the United States Tire Industry, 1920–1937," 30.

the distribution of unit sales between 1921 and 1933; it confirms the pressure on smaller firms. Although information on Goodrich and Fisk is incomplete, it seems likely that the five largest firms increased their overall market share from less than 50 percent in 1921 to over 60 percent in 1929, and to more than 70 percent in 1933. Their combined share rose slightly to 75 percent in 1937.

The fortunes of these big businesses were not uniform. Goodrich and Fisk experienced declining market shares in the late 1920s, with the latter forced down into the category of medium-sized firms. U.S. Rubber also lost ground throughout the 1920s, but then almost tripled its market share in the teeth of the depression between 1929 and 1933. Firestone's market share recovered strongly between 1921 and 1929 but then slipped back. Goodyear reasserted its dominant position following the crisis of 1920–21, and in 1933 the firm's daily capacity of 90,000 casings exceeded the combined capacity of its two nearest rivals.

Table 5.3 considers the entry and exit of firms. The number of new entrants was very high before 1920: 23 percent of the 190 firms operating in 1919 were established in the course of that year. Although enthusiasm was checked by the postwar recession, the formation of new

Table 5.2. Distribution of Unit Tire Sales, 1921–33 (%)

Company	1921	1926	1929	1933
Goodyear	16.1	21.8	29.2	30.1
Firestone	8.2	14.1	19.0	15.4
U.S. Rubber	8.5	7.4	6.6	18.9
B.F. Goodrich	n.a.	10.0	7.2	7.7
Fisk	n.a.	5.3	4.1	3.1
General	n.a.	1.1	1.8	2.7
Dunlop	n.a.	0.8	0.9	1.4
Dayton	n.a.	0.5	0.5	0.7 (1932)
Norwalk	n.a.	0.3 (1927)	0.2	0.4
McCreary	n.a.	n.a.	0.01 (1930)	0.05 (1934)
Seiberling	n.a.	1.3	1.4	1.5
Mohawk Rubber	n.a.	n.a.	0.5 (1930)	0.9

Source: French, "Structural Change and Competition in the United States Tire Industry, 1920–1937," 31.

businesses remained buoyant until the mid-twenties. The failure rate mounted sharply in 1923, however, and remained high throughout the decade, with outright closure being more common than disappearance by merger. After 1929 there were no new entrants.

Inevitably the plethora of new ventures between 1918 and 1921 included many frail enterprises, and the 1920–21 recession magnified any weaknesses and created financial problems. William O'Neil of General Tire asserted contemptuously that the failures "put themselves out of business, they did not belong in business." Certainly there were many brief careers. Ironically, the persistent failure rate encouraged other entrants by creating a stock of secondhand plants and equipment, although such ventures often fared little better.

A few reorganized businesses did succeed. Master Tire and Rubber, forerunner of the present Cooper Tire, developed through a series of reorganizations. McClaren Rubber, created from a defunct company, built up a good trade along the eastern seabord from its North Carolina factory. Frank Seiberling returned to the industry following his ouster from Goodyear. In 1921 Seiberling Rubber was formed through the acquisition of the Lehigh Rubber and Portage Rubber companies. With Seiberling's reputation and his employment of many former Goodyear men, Seiberling Rubber developed into a notable small firm in the

Table 5.3. Entries and Exits in the Tire Industry, 1914–37

Year	New Firms	Failed Companies	Mergers and Acquisitions	Total Exits	Number of Plants	Number of Firms in Operation
1914–18	55	n.a.	n.a.	n.a.	n.a.	n.a.
1919	44	1	0	1	200	190
1920	16	1	1	2	n.a.	n.a.
1921	16	4	5	9	178	n.a.
1922	11	13	3	16	n.a.	166
1923	9	25	4	29	160	129
1924	4	18	4	22	n.a.	111
1925	7	14	4	18	126	97
1926	1	18	2	20	n.a.	93
1927	0	12	1	13	109	92
1928	2	16	2	18	n.a.	78
1929	0	17	2	19	91	62
1930	0	6	5	11	n.a.	50
1931	0	9	2	11	48	n.a.
1932	0	3	0	3	n.a.	n.a.
1933	0	2	0	2	44	35
1934	0	n.a.	n.a.	n.a.	n.a.	n.a.
1935	0	n.a.	2	2	42	n.a.
1936	0	4	2	6	n.a.	n.a.
1937	0	2	1	3	46	n.a.

Source: French, "Structural Change and Competition in the United States Tire Industry, 1920–1937," 33.

replacement market. Seiberling became an advocate of the interests of smaller firms; daily management of the business passed to his son, J. Penfield Seiberling in the late 1920s.

After selling its original U.S. venture in 1898, Dunlop, the leading British tire manufacturer, reappeared in 1923 and opened a plant in Buffalo. The American subsidiary struggled to gain market share and was profitable only in 1926. Two established firms became more prominent. General Tire prospered by concentrating on expensive tires backed by effective marketing and emerged as the principal challenger to the leading producers. More modestly, Armstrong Rubber made its first real advance by purchasing a defunct tire factory in West Haven, Connecticut, in 1922. The firm had been established to manufacture inner tubes in 1912 by George Armstrong, a New Jersey tire dealer, who later sold the business to J. A. Walsh and F. Machlin. Armstrong was to become a significant firm from the late 1930s.

There were opportunities in other tire markets. Production and use of trucks and buses had expanded rapidly since 1909 and received a further stimulus during the war. Between 1921 and 1929 truck and bus production grew from 148,000 to 881,900 vehicles, while total registrations increased from 1.2 million to 3.6 million. This market demanded heavier tires that provided higher prices and profit margins compared with the automobile tire market. Pneumatic tires displaced the earlier reliance on solid tires. The major producers of truck and bus tires, notably Firestone, were prominent in the overall tire business, and OE business and national marketing required an effective after-sales service to truck operators so that new tires were readily available. Nonetheless, truck and bus tires provided a profitable trade for many smaller companies and for retreading firms. Economies of scale were limited because large truck tires required labor-intensive manufacturing methods. The industry also supplied aircraft, bicycle, and motorcycle tires and tubes, as well as repair materials. Manufacturers produced other rubber products, such as footwear, mechanical goods, and waterproofed goods, but these products and other tire markets were dwarfed by the automobile tire business.

The declining number of firms and growing concentration did not simply reflect the weakness of new entrants; rather the 1920s saw fundamental changes in the nature of tire manufacturing. As a result the new entrants faced very different conditions than previously. The divide between the industry leaders and other firms, evident a decade earlier, was accentuated by changes in tire design and marketing. The trends in tire manufacture mirrored to a considerable extent the changing nature and structure of the automobile industry, whose rate of growth slackened.

Changing conditions in the automobile market were fundamental to the tire industry's fortunes. The phase of explosive growth in car sales was replaced by a new susceptibility to fluctuations in demand after 1920. The purchase of automobiles, a durable good, was easily postponed once basic demand had been met, and the growing stock of used cars provided an alternative to a new vehicle. Car manufacturers responded by adopting annual model changes, a form of product differentiation, to promote consumption. Total car output increased substantially over the 1920s, but swings in demand were transmitted to the OE tire market, which represented between one-quarter and one-third of tire sales. After a strong resurgence in 1922 and 1923, OE sales fell 16 percent in 1924, revived in 1925, declined again in the next two years, and then surged to a record 19.9 million tires in 1928 before the first signs of recession depressed orders slightly during 1929.

Changing tire designs placed pressure on small firms. In 1919 three-quarters of tire casings were constructed from cotton fabric impregnated with rubber. Since 1916, however, new high-pressure cord casings and straightside rims had gained ground rapidly through the OE market. In the 1920s these new designs superseded fabric casings. By 1926 fabric casings accounted for only 5.3 percent of sales and within three years were obsolete. High-pressure cords consisted of strands of cotton with few cross threads that allowed closer bonding with the rubber and reduced internal friction. In 1924 high-pressure cords formed nearly 60 percent of all casings produced, but their use then declined as larger and heavier "balloon" cord casings were introduced. The new tire's shape also earned it the nicknames the "doughnut" and the "blimp." In 1929 balloon cords accounted for three-quarters of casings. The major firms pioneered these product innovations, often acquiring textile mills to experiment with cord designs. Balloon tires required adjustments to production processes and used more rubber than previous casings, which increased materials and production costs to the disadvantage of small firms, although there was some compensation from the higher prices and profits on balloon tires.

Straightside rims accounted for only one quarter of all rims in 1919. However, their acceptance accelerated in the late twenties, capturing 87 percent of rim sales in 1929. The market share of the alternative, and previously dominant, clincher rim declined in parallel, and the end of Model T production in 1927 marked the last new car to be equipped with clincher rims. The Model T's earlier popularity ensured the continuing replacement market for some time after 1927, but with the market's eventual decline, small firms were forced to produce new types of tires. Although the cord casing and straightside rim had been well known before 1920, their accelerated acceptance imposed costs on all firms, causing more problems for recent entrants. An exception was Denman-Myers Cord Tire, which was formed in 1919 to produce cord tires and developed into a sound small firm.

Changing tire designs also contributed to major improvements in quality, which altered the relationship between car use and tire demand. Average tire life doubled in the 15 years to 1920 when it reached 5,000 miles. By 1925 a tire lasted for 10,000 miles, and the average rose to 15,000 miles in 1930. Such major advances effectively slowed the growth of the replacement market by lengthening the gap between buying a new car and replacing its tires. The buoyancy of car sales and use sustained the expansion of total tire sales in the 1920s, and balloon tires were more expensive than fabric tires, which raised dollar sales. Yet improved tire life substituted for some potential sales and helped to undermine the hopeful new entrants of 1918 and 1919.

Manufacturing methods also favored increased concentration in the 1920s since the industry became more capital intensive. Open mixing mills were replaced by the Banbury internal mixer, patented in 1916, but not widely used until the twenties. The Banbury's rotor blades mixed rubber and chemicals inside a chamber providing a faster, more controlled mix, a better compound, and savings on labor, power, space, and materials. After 1924 conveyors, chutes, and trucks were used to move materials, partially finished, and finished tires around the factory. This reduced the unskilled workforce in all departments. "Drum" tire building machines, patented by U.S. Rubber in 1919, came into use rapidly between 1923 and 1926 and established the modern form of tire building. On the earlier State machines, the parts of the casing were assembled around a core and, thus, assumed an identifiable tire form before vulcanization. The new machine consisted of a wide drum, around which the casing was built as a flat circular band, thereby reducing tension on the casing during the assembly process. The casing was shaped by being forced around an air or water bag in a vacuum, and the casing and bag were vulcanized together. The drum process made tire building less arduous and improved the uniformity and durability of casings; the machines were not immediately applicable to large truck tires, however.

Banbury mixers, drum machines, and conveyor systems were widely used by the mid-twenties and explain the failure of employment to regain its 1919 peak. In addition, improved chemical accelerators reduced curing times and allowed more intensive use of vulcanizing ovens. Labor turnover was markedly lower after 1922, and the improved retention of skilled labor contributed to efficiency. Overall output per man-hour doubled between 1921 and 1929. From 1914 to 1929 the tire industry led all U.S. manufacturing in terms of growth in output per man-hour. The economist Lloyd Reynolds estimated that maximum economies of scale were achieved from a daily output of 1,000 casings by 1933, while constant returns existed up to 20,000 casings. Such a situation promoted close competition among medium-size and large firms, but further disadvantaged smaller firms and recent entrants.

The prices of rubber and cotton fabrics, which accounted for over half of the industry's costs, were highly volatile in the 1920s. The result was considerable instability, which exacerbated the other pressures on small firms. Small firms purchased monthly supplies of rubber on the "spot" market so that their costs closely reflected current prices. Medium-size companies ordered two or three months ahead, while large manufacturers made forward contracts for between three and six months and purchased overseas. U.S. Rubber, Goodyear, and Firestone acquired rubber plantations, but remained largely dependent on the rubber market and were more cautious in their financial commitments after the inventory losses in 1920–21. In broad terms, if rubber prices rose, small firms soon faced higher costs while their larger rivals were still taking delivery of cheaper rubber. Conversely, declining prices favored smaller companies. Such effects were particularly significant when price changes were large and rapid or coincided with declining tire sales.

In 1922 the British introduced export quotas on southeast Asian rubber supplies, and when a surge in demand followed close on a reduction in the quotas in 1925, prices almost tripled. With their forward contracts, large manufacturers were well placed in the short term, but small firms faced soaring costs. The manager of the tiny Carolina Rubber Company in Salisbury, North Carolina, reported that the firm had to buy rubber on the rising market and "sell their finished goods in competition with other companies who were more fortunate in having contracts at low figures at the beginning of the year" (French, "Structural Change and Competition in the United States Tire Industry, 1920–1937," 35). By contrast Goodyear's large advance orders provided a margin some 25 cents below the 1925 average spot price of 72.5 cents; such an advantage provided windfall profits and a means of delaying tire price increases.

Small and medium-size firms extended their forward purchasing in the expectation that the high prices would be maintained, but then found rubber prices falling by 33 percent in 1926 when shipments increased from nonquota regions. As a result, the unfortunate Carolina Rubber Company now experienced losses on its inventories. The financial costs of fluctuating rubber prices contributed to the failure of twenty firms in 1926 and to the financial weakness of other companies.

The sharp increase in prices in 1925 induced a swing back to greater use of recycled rubber as manufacturers sought a degree of independence from British controls on raw rubber supplies. At this point demand was relatively price-inelastic, and consumption of recycled rubber continued to rise, despite falling rubber prices in 1926 and 1927. By 1928 recycled rubber accounted for one-third of total rubber consumption. The pendulum then swung back from 1929 to 1932 in favor of the natural product, which was cheaper than recycled rubber. Nonetheless, recycled rubber contributed about 20 percent of rubber consumption during the 1930s, giving partial protection from fluctuating rubber prices.

In the early 1920s excess capacity narrowed OE profit margins, and competition forced tire firms to accept the risk of fixed price contracts in 1922. At the same time the tire firms' bargaining position weakened in relation to their OE customers because the number of car producers diminished. By 1929 General Motors, Ford, and Chrysler accounted for 72 percent of car sales and were in a position to force down OE prices. Goodyear and Firestone remained the major suppliers, but in the midtwenties Fisk expanded its sales, and Ford and General Motors offered contracts to medium-size firms such as Mason, Miller, and Kelly-Springfield. The OE market remained highly concentrated: Goodyear accounted for 29 percent, and Firestone for 22 percent of sales around 1929. Yet fluctuating demand, the car firms' bargaining power, and their encouragement of other suppliers ensured a highly competitive market and narrow profit margins.

The replacement market, which accounted for over two-thirds of tire sales, expanded from 28.5 million tires in 1922 to 51.7 million in 1928, before weakening in 1929. Commercial account business, the supply under contract to large purchasers like bus or telephone companies, was a profitable market, but it was characterized by secrecy and suspicion. Manufacturers offered discounts in a haphazard fashion, and from 1927 there were recurring price wars as the major firms competed for national accounts.

As margins fell elsewhere, profits and volume increasingly depended on sales to individual consumers, the most profitable business. Small firms concentrated on the cheapest end of the market, the leading companies sold at the highest prices, and medium-size producers occupied a variety of intermediate positions. These divisions were not absolute: General Tire and Seiberling Rubber were medium-size firms that concentrated on expensive tires. Moreover, in the early 1920s, major producers developed subsidiaries supplying second-line, lower-priced tires, foreshadowing their response to the 1930s depression. In 1923 Goodrich purchased Brunswick Tire, established in 1916, and promoted the Brunswick brand as a second-line tire priced below Goodrich's own tire brands. In 1925 Goodyear purchased the trade name and later the factory of the neighboring Marathon Tire and Rubber Company. Firestone established a subsidiary, the Oldfield Tire Company, in 1923 to supply second-line tires. These moves signaled a weakening of the price structure in the early 1920s, which contributed to the pressure on small firms. In addition, all firms marketed white sidewall tires, which commanded higher prices and emphasized style. The price structure was not rigid. Nonetheless, price movement was broadly parallel because smaller firms often quoted their prices as percentages of Goodyear's wholesale list price. The timing of price changes was a major concern. Any lag in reducing prices risked the loss of sales, while, if rubber prices were increasing, any delay in raising prices might attract orders that would prove unprofitable at the higher level of costs.

Major manufacturers handled the bulk of their own wholesaling, but retailing was firmly the province of independent tire dealers either selling many brands or possessing franchises for particular tire companies. There were a growing number of chains of tire stores as well as auto accessory shops selling tires. For example, Western Auto Supply, formed in 1909 as a mail-order company, entered retailing in 1915 and distributed through branches in major cities. Such larger distributors often purchased tires under their own brand name from producers, and this private or special brand business flourished.

The two preeminent mail-order houses, Montgomery Ward and Sears, Roebuck chose to extend their previously minor tire sales as part of a move into retailing in the 1920s. Sears marketed a "Justice" brand supplied by Murray Rubber, Inland Rubber, and Mason Rubber. However, Sears, dissatisfied with its tire quality and concerned about the financial condition of Murray Rubber, its main supplier, approached Goodyear in 1925. Against the background of volatile rubber prices, a cost-plus contract was negotiated, which, in return for a lower profit margin, protected Goodyear from sudden cost increases and in the event permitted Sears to benefit from declining rubber prices between 1926 and 1929. The original discussions concerned half of Sears's requirements, but at the last moment, Litchfield, soon to become Goodyear's president, captured Sears's entire business by reducing the profit margin from 8 percent to 6 percent. The contract was signed in May 1926, renewed for five years in 1928, and for a further ten years in October 1931. In 1931 the profit margin was raised to 6.5 percent in return for Goodyear's giving between $1.25 and $2 million in common stock and cash to Sears. The Sears's contract testified to Litchfield's determination to strengthen Goodyear's industry leadership by maximizing sales volume. The firm's daily capacity increased from 54,000 tires in 1926 to 89,500 in 1929. Sears pressured Goodyear to establish a southern factory to reduce freight costs to Sears's regional stores, and after some stalling owing to doubts about the scope for lower costs or the need for additional capacity Goodyear established a plant in Gadsden, Alabama, in 1929.

Sears now possessed high-quality tires, marketed under a new Allstate brand, and supported by intensive advertising. Moreover, under the direction of Robert Wood, Sears's retailing expanded from 9 stores in 1926 to 281 in 1929, and tires proved to be the most successful line in its automotive and hardware stores. The Allstate was priced some 25 percent below Goodyear's first-line tire, and thus, it threatened the sales and profit margins of smaller manufacturers and tire dealers. The company had its greatest impact on the low-price end of the market in urban areas, especially on the East Coast.

Montgomery Ward adopted a similar strategy. In 1927 the company purchased tires from Mansfield, Kenyon, Gillette Rubber, and Samson Tire and Rubber. The four firms were based in Ohio, New Jersey, Wisconsin, and California, respectively, and were selected to provide national distribution. In 1931 Montgomery Ward divided its tire business on a cost-plus basis between Goodrich and U.S., Rubber; the latter absorbed Gillette and Samson to maintain effective distribution. The two mail-order firms' combined share of tire sales expanded from 8.8 percent in 1926 to 18.3 percent in 1929.

Small manufacturers tried to maintain their prices below Sears's level, and medium-size companies compensated dealers for extra discounts where necessary to meet the competition. Firestone used second-line tires to meet Sears's prices, and other large and medium-size producers further extended their use of second lines, often through subsidiaries, to satisfy anxious dealers. The result was a range of prices and qualities with a greater emphasis on the cheaper end of the market, adding to the financial difficulties of smaller companies. Although the entry of the mail-order firms was a major stimulus to price cutting, it was not the only factor. Local price wars erupted periodically, often triggered by the increasingly common regional price cutting for commercial account orders. The California market was particularly prone to these outbreaks following the establishment of local factories by Goodyear, Firestone, and Goodrich. Firestone's entry in 1927, and the excess capacity in the local industry ensured intense competition in California.

Leading manufacturers responded to private brands and mass distribution by entering retailing directly through the establishment of company stores. Table 5.4 shows the pattern of store ownership by firm. Often these were existing dealerships that the tire firm either purchased outright or took a financial stake in. Firestone launched an "M and M"—majority and minority interest—program in 1928 whereby the manufacturer owned 51 percent and the dealer 49 percent of each store. Firestone increased its capitalization to finance further expansion. Significantly, Firestone, lacking special brand business, pursued the most vigorous retail stores policy, and Goodyear and Goodrich also built up a significant retail presence in urban markets. U.S. Rubber Company, through its Quick Tire subsidiaries, possessed a handful of stores but, in contrast to the other leading manufacturers, discontinued most of its retail outlets between 1930 and 1934; by 1939 U.S. Rubber had sold its retail outlets. Most medium-size producers avoided retailing, although Dunlop's spectacular program reflected its multinational ambitions. General Tire achieved steady, if modest, expansion, but Fisk Rubber could not sustain its stores. Among smaller firms, Carolina Rubber opened one store, which proved a burden, and Dayton Rubber's stores were closed after 1929. For other small producers the strategy of entering tire retailing was simply too expensive.

Overall the industry was in a state of flux during the 1920s. Despite increased sales and spectacular productivity growth, competition increased and the number of producers diminished significantly. The automobile sector as a whole became vulnerable to the postponement of purchases, and fluctuating OE demand created periodic unused production capacity and excess inventories among leading tire firms. Even the expansion of replacement demand was less than anticipated by new entrants in 1919 because improved tire life slowed sales. Smaller companies were weakened by the post war recession, volatile rubber prices in the mid-twenties, and the expense of introducing balloon tires. Meanwhile innovations in products and production methods strengthened the leading producers. Still the existence of constant returns across a broad range of output levels ensured considerable competition. The price structure, weakened by the 1920–21 recession, was destabilized by the growth of private brand business, especially following the 1926 Sears contract. Friction was evident in Goodyear's determination to expand sales and Harvey Firestone's bitter reaction to competition from Sears.

Table 5.4. Number of Retail Stores by Firm, 1924–35

Year	Firestone	Goodyear	U.S. Rubber	B. F. Goodrich	General	Fisk	Dunlop	Dayton
1924	0	5	0	n.a.	2	0	0	n.a.
1926	3	22	n.a.	n.a.	2	n.a.	n.a.	12
1927	9	28	n.a.	n.a.	4	n.a.	n.a.	n.a.
1928	62	45	n.a.	n.a.	9	n.a.	n.a.	n.a.
1929	337	98	24	109	14	n.a.	n.a.	n.a.
1930	430	134	n.a.	150	22	121	20	n.a.
1931	399	191	n.a.	169	25	n.a.	n.a.	n.a.
1932	374	233	n.a.	144	29	n.a.	n.a.	n.a.
1933	371	224	n.a.	152	32	n.a.	n.a.	n.a.
1934	423	262	19	n.a.	36	3	510	1
1935	n.a.	n.a.	n.a.	n.a.	41	n.a.	n.a.	n.a.

Source: French, "Structural Change and Competition in the United States Tire Industry, 1920–1937," 41.

These uncertainties presented genuine difficulties and depressed profits, which prompted a search for new strategies. In 1927 prominent industrialists, including the Du Pont family, which had obtained control of U.S. Rubber in 1927, considered merging U.S. Rubber, Goodyear, and Seiberling to create a powerful industry leader; financial institutions and major shareholders had been dissatisfied with the industry's poor profits since the early 1920s. The merger scheme foundered due to doubts about raising equity capital, fears of antitrust action, and Litchfield's belief that the Sears contract would consolidate Goodyear's own dominance.

The industry then attempted to follow a cooperative approach. The established trade association, the Rubber Association of America, was bypassed because Firestone, the second largest firm, had withdrawn in 1923 because of disagreements over policy toward British rubber restrictions. Instead the Rubber Institute was created in June 1928; a majority of manufacturers enrolled, and the institute's 15 directors were drawn equally from large, medium, and small companies. The institute was rooted firmly in the trade association movement and the cooperative policies of the Federal Trade Commission in the 1920s. Formal approval of policies was to be obtained from federal agencies, and Lincoln Andrews, the institute's director-general, argued that cooperation would forestall oligopoly and antitrust action. Published price lists and codes of trade ethics were planned to foster "wholesome competition," with the institute coordinating information sharing. Separate conferences were established for six product divisions in July 1928, and the ten producers of OE tires discussed pricing policies and a code of business practice. The first test came in the autumn of 1928 when the 1929 contracts were made. The result was immediate failure, and the code was abandoned by November 1928. Competition in the OE and commercial account markets had intensified from the mid-1920s, and the attractions of volume contracts inhibited agreement on prices and sales methods. In the replacement market, the growth of private brand business and the dealers' independence rendered the institute powerless. Under Litchfield's direction, Goodyear pursued a resolute policy of expanding market share in the late 1920s and was more aggressive once the financial and managerial influence of the 1921 refinancing had been overcome. Harvey Firestone was similarly independent and irascible, especially in response to Sears's expansion, and there was, thus, little room for industrywide cooperation. Andrews tried to sustain the Rubber Institute by strengthening its links with the Rubber Manufacturers' Association (formerly the Rubber Association of America), but the industry regarded the institute as a broken reed, and it was dissolved in May 1929.

6

The Industry in Depression, 1929–1940

FROM THE ONSET OF THE DEPRESSION IN 1929, real incomes slumped 35 percent by 1933. This particularly affected demand for durable goods such as automobiles. As a result OE tire sales contracted by two-thirds, and, with the loss of business resulting in underemployed factories, OE suppliers reduced tire prices to all car makers in an effort to maximize sales. Fisk and several medium-size producers were squeezed out of the market, but at the same time, U.S. Rubber dramatically increased its OE market share from 6.9 percent in 1929 to 30 percent in 1931. A contributing factor was Du Pont's interest in both U.S. Rubber and General Motors. When Du Pont acquired control of U.S. Rubber in 1927, Irenee du Pont favored selling its unprofitable tire division, but Francis B. Davis, the company's new president, advocated continuation. Production was concentrated in Detroit, and the key breakthrough came with a contract for half of General Motors's OE business in 1931. U.S. Rubber also substantially increased sales to Ford.

Initially GM financed cotton and rubber purchases for its tires, and a 1933 contract with U.S. Rubber assured that all tires made for GM would be supplied on the basis of the lowest price offered by any other OE supplier. The car firm had considered producing its own tires until a study in 1930 concluded that OE tires could be purchased at below factory cost. Ford operated a tire plant at River Rouge between 1938 and 1943 before selling the equipment to the Soviet Union, but it still relied primarily on tire suppliers. The contraction of OE sales left industry leaders more reliant on replacement business to use manufacturing capacity, spread overhead costs, and make profits. Meanwhile U.S. Rubber's resurgence placed additional pressure on Goodyear and Firestone.

In the commercial account market, the depression also intensified competition. Firestone launched a campaign of confidential discounts in 1929, and the major manufacturers cut prices aggressively. Medium-size firms found their accounts threatened and, in turn, sought local contracts, previously regarded as trivial, from small producers. All firms supported their dealers and salesmen with discounts or special terms; by 1932 large buyers were purchasing, in effect, on a bid basis. Between 1926 and 1932 commercial account business was conducted at a loss. Competition in one regional market could affect other markets as occurred in 1930 when a West Coast price war spread nationally.

Replacement sales fell by one-third from 1929 to 1932, with the contraction concentrated in 1930 and 1932. Although less drastic in relative terms, the absolute fall in replacement business slightly exceeded that in OE sales. In 1930 car registrations and average mileage increased, but motorists delayed tire purchases. By 1932 depressed replacement demand reflected the earlier fall in car sales, the longer life of balloon cords, and declining vehicle use. Tires were not only linked to automobile sales and use and, thus, to one of the most depressed sectors in the 1930s, but were themselves at least semidurable and hence vulnerable to postponed purchasing.

The depression's swift impact brought the most significant failures and acquisitions of the interwar years. Mason Tire and Rubber encountered financial problems in 1928 and, despite a reorganization, went bankrupt a year later. Michelin closed its American factory in 1930. Other middling companies were bought out by leading firms. Goodrich acquired Hood Rubber (1929) and Miller Rubber (1930), while U.S. Rubber absorbed two small firms, Gillette Tire and Rubber (1930) and Samson Tire and Rubber (1931), and later purchased Fisk (1940). Fisk, a declining power throughout the 1920s, was in the hands of a receiver from 1931 to 1933. Kelly-Springfield went into bankruptcy in 1934 and was taken over by Goodyear a year later. General Tire bought Yale Tire and Rubber in 1931 and later added India Tire and Rubber. Finally, Lee Tire and Rubber acquired Republic in 1936. These acquisitions sustained the rising level of concentration in the industry and, though triggered by the depression, originated in the structural changes of the late twenties.

The immediate response of surviving firms of all sizes was contraction. Total employment declined from 83,263 in 1929 to 49,159 two years later, wages and salaries were cut, and manufacturers adopted six-hour shifts and four-day weeks. The pace of innovations was slowed by excess capacity and reduced investment. In the atmosphere of dismissals output per man-hour increased sharply between 1929 and 1931, but thereafter productivity growth stagnated.

The retrenchment was a watershed in Akron's standing. The city's share of total U.S. tire capacity peaked at 66 percent in 1930. Goodyear, Firestone, and Goodrich already possessed California plants and from the mid-thirties pursued a deliberate policy of dispersing production outside Ohio. Akron's tradition of high wages became a source of dissatisfacton, but managements also reacted to the emergence of the United Rubber Workers union, which was most powerful in Akron.

The tire industry's labor relations in the 1930s have been analyzed by historian Daniel Nelson ("Managers and Nonunion Workers", *Industrial and Labor Relations Review*, October 1989, 41–52). After 1909 Goodyear's extensive employee welfare scheme had developed into the Industrial Assembly, an internal system of employee representation that retained the support of a large number of workers even during the union organizing drives of the 1930s. Litchfield's determined resistance limited union influence before 1941 but contributed to a weakening of Goodyear's industrial leadership. The firm's productivity declined, and after the end of the Sears contract Goodyear's marketing was less innovative. Firestone and Goodrich operated welfare schemes and established company unions in reaction to the passage of the National Industrial Recovery Act in 1933. These new company unions soon collapsed, but Firestone and Goodrich resisted union influence while attempting to maintain output and accelerated their longer-term strategy of dispersion to new plants. The URW made its greatest gains at U.S. Rubber and General Tire where managers were more conciliatory. Nelson shows that smaller producers were usually singlemindedly antiunion. During the 1930s independent unions achieved a remarkable breakthrough in the tire industry compared with their earlier marginal role. Nevertheless, membership gains were often not translated into employer recognition of union bargaining, and membership fell during the 1937–38 recession. The character of labor relations was only finally shaped in the war economy.

As rubber prices collapsed from 20.6 cents per pound in 1929 to only 3.5 cents per pound in 1932, the leading firms sustained massive inventory losses. On the marketing side major companies abandoned their smallest dealers and reduced their sales force: U.S. Rubber ceased sales in towns with less than one thousand car registrations, and Fisk discontinued two-thirds of its dealerships by excluding those with less than $200 in annual sales. Smaller firms curtailed their sales area. Norwalk Tire and Rubber distributed nationally until 1930, but then restricted sales to within 250 miles of its Connecticut plant. Dayton closed twelve branches in 1928, reducing its dealers from 1,434 to 139. The many failures and the larger firms' retrenchment allowed some smaller companies to expand their local or regional business, and this niche was reflected in increased market shares for the Norwalk, McCreary, and Mohawk companies.

Goodyear, Firestone, Goodrich, Dunlop, and, to a lesser degree, General Tire used company retail outlets to continue their penetration of major urban markets. By 1930 Firestone had 430 stores and bought out most of its M and M dealers that remained after the onslaught of the depression. Goodyear's stores increased from 98 in 1929 to 233 in 1932, and Goodyear Service Inc. established garages that retailed tires. The number of Goodrich's Silvertown stores expanded from 109 to 144 between 1929 and 1932. Dunlop's stores increased their sales from 36,000 tires through 20 stores in 1929 to 204,599 tires through over 400 stores in 1932.

Company stores operated at a loss in the early 1930s. In the case of Goodyear, a retail operating committee in Akron established prices for all of the firm's stores. Independent dealers who bought from Goodyear received discounts that were related to the quantity of tires purchased. Goodyear's own stores received the maximum discount irrespective of turnover and were therefore highly competitive. Between 1926 and 1933 Goodyear's stores showed a net loss of around $9.4 million. Most of Dunlop's stores were in the red, and Firestone's stores incurred some $7 million in losses, despite the introduction of gasoline, batteries, spark plugs, and car accessories in a bid to achieve some profit. Such large and persistent losses resulted, in large part, from the depressed state of demand and the search for volume regardless of margins. In addition, the stores were used to bid for local commercial account business, a highly competitive sector. Since company stores' share of replacement sales increased from 4.4 percent in 1929 to 11 percent in 1933, the major firms' ability to carry the financial burden of retail stores was a significant advantage.

Yet the most successful firm in the replacement market of the 1930s owed little or nothing to retail stores. U.S. Rubber had pioneered involvement in retailing as early as 1912 and possessed 20 Quick Tire subsidiaries operating 22 service stations by the mid-twenties. Further outlets were added, but the reduction in the firm's dealers was accompanied by the closure of all but two Quick Tire companies between 1930 and 1934. The Tire Division's subsequent proposals for a retail store program were rejected by the board; by 1939 the firm had no stores. Yet U.S. Rubber's share of total replacement sales increased from an average of 7 percent in the 1920s to 15 percent in 1932, and to 31 percent by

1940. As a result, the company challenged Goodyear and Firestone for the first time in two decades. U.S. Rubber benefited from Davis's reorganization of the tire division, the spin-offs from its GM contract, and substantial sales to Montgomery Ward and oil companies. Davis's strategy depended on the low prices and narrow profit margins necessary in OE and private-brand markets, and this was reflected in consistent, if diminishing, losses between 1928 and 1934.

The structure of marketing continued to undergo change. Oil companies moved into tire retailing and increased their replacement market share from 1 percent in 1929 to 10 percent in 1934, as shown in Table 6.1. Small firms captured some of this trade, but U.S. Rubber, Goodrich, and Goodyear dominated this new outlet for replacement tire sales. In 1929–30 U.S. Rubber and Goodrich signed contracts to supply tires to Western Auto Supply, Colonial Beacon, and Atlas Supply (the last two were subsidiaries of Standard Oil companies). The tire producers supplied tires for sales through the oil companies' established network of gas stations. U.S. Rubber, in particular, was able to use the outlets of mass distributors to strengthen its replacement tire business. Conversely, Firestone obtained few private brand orders and relied on its own stores and independent dealers.

Wholesale list prices fell by one-quarter between 1929 and 1932,

Table 6.1. Distribution of Replacement Tire Sales by Outlet, 1926–37 (%)

Year	Independent Dealers	Mail Order	Company Retail Stores	Oil Companies
1926	91.2	8.8	0	0
1927	90.5	9.5	0	0
1928	86.3	12.9	0.8	0
1929	76.2	18.3	4.4	1.1
1930	72.5	16.8	8.1	2.6
1931	70.5	14.0	10.3	5.2
1932	68.8	14.2	10.3	6.7
1933	65.9	14.7	11.0	8.4
1934	65.0	15.0	10.0	10.0
1937	53.0	19.0	11.0	17.0

Sources: For 1926–33, U.S., National Recovery Administration, *History of the Code of Fair Competition for the Retail Rubber Tire and Battery Code*, 3, table 2; for 1934–37, Gaffey, *The Productivity of Labor in the Rubber Tire Manufacturing Industry*, 57.

but this decline did not reflect the true extent and nature of price competition. As the depression worsened, a rigid pattern of sales developed: a spring peak and a pronounced low in autumn and winter, which encouraged pricecutting late in the year. All manufacturers adopted second-, third-, and even fourth-line tires in order to reduce prices and tire quality in the competitive struggle. According to one Firestone dealer, second and third lines accounted for 58 percent of sales in 1933 compared to 8 percent in 1929. The structure of prices became compressed. For example, the differential between Goodyear's first line All-Weather tire and Sears's Allstate brand narrowed from 25 percent in 1930 to 10 percent in 1934 even though both supplier and distributor wished to preserve a greater differential. Both introduced second lines: Sears's Crusader and Goodyear's Pathfinder. Firestone priced second- and third-line tires at Sears's level, and small firms priced their first-line tires to compete with the mail-order companies. Manufacturers offered extended warranties, special trade-in terms, and free inner tubes, while confidential discounts to customers and rebates to dealers increased steadily.

Such practices were encouraged by anxious dealers wishing to compete with mass distributors or local rivals, and they imposed a financial strain that was compounded by losses and the growing banking crisis. Indeed bank holidays early in 1933 compelled Seiberling to close temporarily because "there was no use in trying to sell goods when dealers could not pay for them in anything that we could use" (F. A. Seiberling to M. W. Harrison, 15 March 1933, F. A. Seiberling Papers, Box 71, Ohio Historical Society). The shrinkage of price differentials placed the greatest pressure on medium-size firms occupying the middle range of prices. They were threatened both by cheaper private brands and by price-cutting on leading manufacturers' brands. As a result several middle-size companies disappeared in the 1930s. The price structure explains both the declining number of small manufacturers and the ability of a few to survive. On the one hand, price differentials narrowed, and at times collapsed, in the struggle for volume, which weakened the small firms. On the other hand, small producers used discounts to resist a total invasion of their local territories and price ranges.

The scale of the depression, the divisions between manufacturers and retailers, and the entry of the oil companies into the tire business prevented any cooperation among producers between 1929 and 1931. In the winter of 1930–31 tentative discussions of pricing policy were cut short when Goodyear and Sears reduced prices. The further contraction of demand in 1932 aggravated the industry's crisis. Early that year the major manufacturers had to forgo higher prices to remain competitive with the mass distributors.

The fundamental conflicts were evident in the industry's response to the federal Revenue Act, which imposed a tax on tires and tubes in June 1932. Some smaller firms saw the tax as an ideal opportunity for a general price increase. Yet manufacturers extended credit to dealers who ordered at pretax prices and, thus, created stocks that undermined future efforts to raise prices. U.S. Rubber, Firestone, and Sears then decided not to pass the tax on to customers, compelling other firms to absorb the financial burden. Moreover, Goodyear, the industry leader, used only 48 percent of its Akron capacity in 1932 and responded by selling tires at the cost of production by late summer and using further discounts to support dealers in local price wars. Competition was acute on the West Coast where Goodyear's Los Angeles plant operated at only 27 percent of capacity in 1933. The struggle for volume in a diminishing market was costly and financial resources, stretched by the long depression and an increasingly frail commercial banking system, were crucial. In September 1932, Firestone and Sears finally agreed to raise prices to cover the tax, but bankers and major shareholders failed in their efforts to promote further increases or general agreement on prices and output.

In January 1933 the Rubber Manufacturers' Association, the principal trade association, proposed a scheme for maintaining list prices, while sales managers examined specific complaints in the most competitive markets. A. L. Viles, RMA president, reported that prices were "more thoroughly demoralized" than ever before, with some dealers offering discounts between 50 percent and 60 percent below list prices. The RMA plan foundered when Firestone introduced a 10 percent reduction to meet Sears's prices. This was the nadir of the depression, and price cutting recurred throughout the spring. In March Goodyear, U.S. Rubber, Goodrich, and Sears agreed to limit their use of cheaper tires and accept a 10 percent margin between first-line and mail-order prices, but Firestone still insisted on meeting Sears's prices. Other firms reduced their lines, but effectively retained the same prices by extending discounts to cash customers. The net result was that manufacturers had to rebate their dealers on orders made at higher prices during the winter. Over a 40-day period, McClaren Rubber rebated $60,000 to dealers as compensation for lower prices at a time when the bank holiday crisis was at its height.

A few optimistic signs appeared between March and June 1933. Business was stimulated by the stabilization of commercial banking and a general business upturn in anticipation of the passage of the National

Industrial Recovery Act. The leading firms agreed on higher prices in April 1933, although there was criticism that small firms had not received adequate notice of the new prices. With the beginnings of a recovery in automobile production, OE tire sales revived in 1933 and within three years had surpassed their 1929 level. The 1937–38 recession cut OE sales by half, but demand then rose strongly to 1941. This post-1932 resurgence benefited the large manufacturers who dominated the OE market, although OE sales remained less profitable than either replacement or commercial account business.

Such elements of recovery were, however, offset by the declining state of the replacement market in which sales fell continuously between 1929 and 1935. In the latter year replacement sales were 59 percent of their 1929 level and even by 1939 represented only 76 percent of 1929 sales. This sluggish performance maintained pressure on manufacturers and retailers. The persistent weakness of replacement sales, the many failures, and the ineffectual private lobbying for higher prices explain the willingness of small and medium-size manufacturers to seek protection through the National Recovery Administration (NRA) after June 1933. A Tire Code Committee for manufacturers was established under the chairmanship of A. L. Viles, and a separate Retail Tire Code was organized under the auspices of the National Tire Dealers Association (NTDA). In essence, the industry wanted higher prices to improve profits, and this aim was given added weight by general increases in labor and raw material costs after 1933.

There were considerable obstacles to any agreement. First, and most fundamental, was the unused capacity resulting from weak replacement demand. A second issue was the relationship between prices and costs. Rubber prices increased sharply in 1933 and 1934, albeit from an abnormally low base. Although small firms soon incurred higher costs, larger companies had accumulated stocks at depression prices, and Goodyear was particularly well placed. In 1933 Frank Seiberling believed Goodyear had sufficient reserves of 3 cent rubber for two years, while smaller producers were already paying 9 cents. The advantage would dimimish, but it benefited larger manufacturers with huge stocks. Any price agreement had to consider whether prices should be set on the basis of the historic cost of raw materials or market replacement cost. Despite opposition from Goodyear, Goodrich, and U.S. Rubber, the NRA Tire Code Committee decided to draft a standard cost accounting manual to determine average costs. Viles regarded the manual as the key to any cooperation. Yet lengthy discussions failed to produce any agreement on raw material costs or on the vexing questions about establishing production costs and profit margins. Other NRA codes encountered similar problems, but they were particularly acute in the tire business because manufacturing combined capital-intensive production with substantial raw material costs.

A third problem was the price structure. On the one hand, there was the relationship between the prices of large, medium, and small manufacturers, and on the other hand, there were the divisions in the retail sector between mail-order firms, oil companies, manufacturers' stores, and independent dealers. To be effective, any policy had to be enforced in both the manufacturing and the retail codes. With contracting demand and excess capacity, all manufacturers and retailers had every incentive to obtain business by cutting prices. The first discussions were among manufacturers. A Tire Code Authority discussed proposals for a sales quota covering OE and replacement tires, but this was rejected following opposition from Firestone and Fisk. Instead the Code Authority suggested a 90-day plan for price differentials that divided manufacturers into four sections according to size. At the code hearings, Levy of Fisk demanded a pricing policy based on a cost manual rather than predetermined differentials and refused to concede lower prices to mail-order firms. Goodyear's sales manager, Robert Wilson, expressed the opposition of Goodyear, Goodrich, U.S. Rubber, and four minors to the plan. Wilson pointed out that general controls would not reflect the varying importance of individual firms in particular markets.

This opposition succeeded in deleting the price scheme from the draft code, through 20 small and medium-size firms then objected to the absence of any provisions for price differentials or a cost accounting manual. NRA officials wanted a code acceptable to a majority of firms, and eventually Frank Seiberling broke the impasse by persuading 19 small firms and two large companies to agree on a draft code covering tire producers. It was approved on Christmas Day 1933. The Tire Code left the basic issues unresolved: current prices were to be maintained for 90 days and plans for some form of price agreement or market stabilization were to be submitted within 60 days. In effect, the divisions that inhibited broad agreement remained; list prices were little more than notional, and the industry's hopes for some relief now focused on the separate Retail Rubber Tire and Battery Trade Code.

Generally, NRA codes were drafted by an appropriate trade association, discussed in a public hearing, and finally approved by the federal government. The operation of each code was left to a code authority that represented those involved in the particular business. Often the trade association played the key role in establishing and implementing the code. The central role of the RMA in the code for tire manufacturing provides an example of a trade association's coordinating role in an NRA code, albeit in a discordant industry. There were even greater divisions in the case of the Retail Rubber Tire and Battery Trade Code. The prime mover of the Retail Code was the National Tire Dealers' Association [NTDA], a poorly financed and loosely organized body that had grown out of numerous local associations formed since 1927 in response to the rise of mass distributors. The NTDA was composed of small independent dealers. Its role was resented by some of the larger dealers operating multiple stores. An even greater problem was that the NTDA did not encompass other types of tire retailers such as manufacturers' retail stores, mail-order firms, oil companies, and chain stores. The Retail Code Authority, however, had to include representatives of all of these important groups as well as the NTDA, and there was little common ground among the different parties. NTDA revived the proposal for agreed price differentials that were based on the list price of the leading manufacturers and granted lower prices to small producers and mass distributors. Firestone and Fisk restated their opposition. Levy argued that such predetermined differentials would give control over all prices to the large firms through their list prices, and he refused to concede any advantage to private brands. Levy again advocated some form of cost accounting manual. Firestone attacked the influence of mail-order and chain stores in the Code Authority, while chain stores opposed any controls on prices or warranties. The debate emphasized the industry's divisions and the barriers to any cooperative strategy.

After the code hearings, conferences on the final version of the Retail Code continued for the first three months of 1934 against the unpromising background of a general price war. In January 1934 Sears introduced a 25 percent discount for buyers who traded in tires; the industry followed suit, and a planned return to list prices lasted barely a week. Frank Seiberling led a group of small manufacturers who lobbied assiduously in Washington for the enforcement of higher prices and agreed differentials, but the NRA administrators initially refused to countenance fixed differentials. Sears sustained its sales campaign. A 40-day truce was arranged in April, although local price wars persisted, and a control committee was established in Akron. This was essentially a complaints committee, which sought to raise prices or investigate advertising campaigns in specific areas, although company representatives often simply defended their dealer's actions. Meanwhile, sales managers continued to authorize further discounts to meet local conditions. Smaller firms questioned the major companies' commitment to the control committee and continued to seek federal action. Cost accounting manuals were drafted, discussed, and ignored, while price controls were canvassed and condemned.

Then, in early May the NRA issued an administrative order establishing minimum prices under a system of price filing. The order was based on Goodyear's February 1934 price list with a three-tier structure allowing lower prices for mail-order and private brand tires. Guarantees were to be held constant, and manufacturers agreed to discontinue free offers and rebates to dealers. The NRA justified the order as protection for the small dealer against "destructive price cutting" by larger distributors.

The administrative order was in effect until October 1934, but had limited impact. Leon Henderson, director of the NRA's Research and Planning Division, was to handle complaints of noncompliance. If a dispute was not resolved within 48 hours, all parties were entitled to meet the competition through lower prices. The mail-order houses had already printed summer catalogs advertising prices below agreed levels, and NRA's acceptance of these prices discredited the administrative order. A Retail Tire Code Authority was appointed in late May, and its sessions featured persistent arguments over alleged violations of price and trade practice provisions. In practice, the declared price structure had collapsed with the minimum prices effectively becoming the maximum price level. Goodyear, Firestone, and Fisk matched mail-order prices with at least one line. In general, the structure of tire markets promoted deviations from list prices and NRA codes. The only cooperation came in major markets such as New York, Chicago, and San Francisco, where the five leading firms sought agreement through the control committee and accepted some loss of sales to small producers and dealers.

A group of small and medium-size manufacturers, led by Seiberling Rubber, attempted to coordinate lobbying for a 5 percent to 10 percent margin below the large companies' prices. This triumph of desperation over experience proved ineffective because other small producers sold private brands at lower prices. The companies were also divided between those emphasising price differentials and others that placed their faith in the elusive cost accounting manual. J. W. Whitehead, president of Norwalk Tire and Rubber, complained that the interests of the small companies "are just as much at variance among themselves as with the large companies" (J. W. Whitehead to J. Penfield Seiberling, 27 June 1934, J. Penfield Seiberling Papers, Ohio Historical Society Collection 824).

When the administrative order expired in October 1934, the manufacturing and retail codes were in chaos, and no progress had been made on pricing policy. The idea of a vertical code linking tire manufacturing and retailing had been rejected as impractical. The NTDA and some small manufacturers requested a continuation of the emergency provisions to protect independent dealers, but demanded effective federal enforcement. Large manufacturers, mail-order firms, and oil companies opposed further NRA price fixing, and federal officials, disillusioned with the Retail Tire Code, allowed the administrative order to lapse, marking the end of any federal impulse for cooperation.

The control committee of sales managers in Akron continued to respond to specific local disputes through ad hoc arrangements in major markets. Manufacturers increasingly blamed instability on price cutting by dealers and attempted to persuade their own dealers to maintain prices. Yet local disputes often originated in the commercial account market where producers promoted discounting and the control committee's influence was limited. In December 1934 the industry agreed to terminate all commercial account contracts that were priced below a certain level and sought to agree on standard bids for government business. Yet continuing surplus capacity ensured that discounting and warranty competition persisted.

In May 1935 the Supreme Court's decision in the Schechter case brought an end to the NRA. The Rubber Manufacturers' Association decided to continue seeking cooperation in "all lawful ways." Proposals to use U.S. Rubber as a price leader foundered on the old issue of enforcement. That autumn Goodyear and Firestone embarked on further price cutting. Attitudes appear to have altered, however, by 1936 when Frank Seiberling and Harvey Firestone considered prices more stable than at any time in the 1930s. Goodyear's president, Paul Litchfield, advocated "profits before volume," and the control committee made a new effort to obtain agreement on prices and trade practices. Sales managers renewed their pressure on dealers that ignored list prices. The greater stability was primarily due to a rise in replacement sales, the first increase since 1929, which improved capacity utilization to 83 percent. Major producers also benefited from the continued recovery in OE sales. On the supply side, the failure and acquisitions of medium-size firms had reduced competition, and more significantly Goodyear's contract with Sears was canceled six years before its scheduled termination. The Federal Trade Commission had been investigating the contract since 1934 and issued a "cease and desist" order in April 1936. Goodyear had argued that the low price granted to Sears represented a reasonable allowance for its volume purchasing. The FTC decision asserted, however, that any price discrimination had to be confined to savings made in marketing and shipping tires not in manufacturing, and thus, Sears's price was too low.

The case hinged on differing interpretations of the Clayton Act, but Congress then passed the Robinson-Patman Act, which was intended to protect small retailers in general from the competition of chain stores. In this atmosphere Goodyear and Sears decided against challenging the FTC's ruling. The cancellation of the contract removed a major source of friction between Goodyear and Firestone and explains Litchfield's new emphasis on profits. By 1939 several firms were supplying Sears, although the Armstrong Rubber Company obtained the major share of the business. This marked the beginning of a continuing business relationship, which turned Armstrong into a significant force in the industry. Sears provided financial support for the construction of a modern factory at Natchez, Mississippi, in 1938, although Armstrong later bought out Sears's investment.

The stability of list prices carried over into 1937 when several firms attempted to use state fair trade laws to enforce minimum prices and instituted resale price maintenance in California. Yet the quiet trading conditions proved merely a lull. The U.S. economy entered a severe recession in the spring of 1937, which lasted almost twelve months. The downturn was felt most in the OE market where sales in 1938 were barely half their 1937 level. Replacement business was checked during 1937, but rose slightly in the following year. Overall the industry used only 53 percent of its capacity in 1938. The slump in demand and the continuing increase in the market share of mail-order, chain store, and oil companies revived competition. A survey of the Atlanta dealers in 1938 revealed extensive discounting: only 6.2 percent of tires were sold at list price and nearly 42 percent retailed at discounts ranging from 20 percent to 45 percent.

During the 1930s manufacturers gave greater attention to other products since the automobile tire market was so weak. Truck and bus tire sales declined in the early 1930s, with a sharp fall in OE sales in 1932, but replacement sales of truck tires rose after 1931. Aggressive marketing and the buying power of large users restricted profits, especially after General Tire's entry into the business in 1928. Goodyear and Firestone developed a range of pneumatic tires for tractors, farm machinery, and earth-moving equipment. Harvey Firestone, like his friend and major customer Henry Ford, took a keen personal interest in the mechanization of farming. These markets developed steadily, but required considerable research effort. Goodyear also continued its production of aircraft tires and airships.

As the economy recovered in 1934 mechanical goods sales improved, and since research and production costs were low, smaller firms found mechanical and molded goods a profitable trade. Dayton Rubber's profits came primarily from its sales of transmission belting. Goodyear, Firestone, and Goodrich increasingly located mechanical goods production in lower wage plants away from Akron. Manufacturers also developed car accessories such as engine mountings and seat covers. Firestone began manufacturing spark plugs and batteries to stock in its stores. On the other hand, Seiberling's car accessory business proved small and unprofitable, and General Tire's management prohibited its stores from carrying car accessories. Firms also gave greater attention to their research laboratories and chemicals divisions and made progress in developing new materials, such as latex foams. But this aspect did not have a major impact on sales until the 1940s.

The scale of the depression between 1929 and 1932 swiftly reduced automobile sales and the derived demand for tires. As in 1920–21, manufacturers responded by contracting their workforces, achieving short-term productivity gains, reducing wages, promoting cheaper lines, and extending their use of special deals. In this capital-intensive industry, substantial unusued capacity ensured price cutting in bids to maximize volume; financial pressures, aggravated by an unstable banking system, hastened the collapse of small and medium-size firms. The entry of oil companies into tire retailing also accelerated the growth of private brand business at the expense of independent dealers.

Although foreshadowed by the postwar recession and the structural changes of the 1920s, the protracted fall in replacement sales in the 1930s made the industry's position acute. When private efforts, notably through the Rubber Manufacturers' Association, failed to raise prices, the trade association and some small and medium-size firms sought agreement through the NRA. Although in the main antagonistic to the New Deal or skeptical of its effectiveness, the industry eventually obtained manufacturing and retail codes and a federal administrative order controlling prices. Private efforts were also made to regulate competition.

Yet divisions among manufacturers, the complexity of the retail sector, and the weakness of demand combined to prevent effective agreement on prices or trade practices. By the late thirties the recovery of demand had brought a degree of stability, but it remained fragile and vulnerable to the 1937–38 recession, winter price cutting, and conflicts among producers, dealers, and private brands. The industry had attained a degree of maturity. Many of the pioneers had left the scene. Harvey Firestone died in 1938, and Frank Seiberling was in semi-retirement. Two long-serving executives remained in leading positions, Litchfield at Goodyear and John W. Thomas at Firestone. Family control was to continue at Firestone, General Tire, and Seiberling Rubber, but Davis's revitalization of U.S. Rubber and Litchfield's role at Goodyear pointed to the trend toward career managers. Production was dominated by five large firms, and the structure and volatility of the replacement market were established. Both the concentration of production and the volatility of replacement sales were to be evident after 1945, but World War II changed the industry dramatically in the short term and introduced new longer-term influences.

7

World War II

IN 1939 AND 1940 THE U.S. FINALLY BEGAN
to shake off the protracted depression, and economic activity quickened.
The outbreak of war in Europe created both an economic stimulus and
new uncertainties. The limited American efforts at preparedness planning lacked urgency and commitment, but after Pearl Harbor they were
succeeded by increasing mobilization of the economy. The sudden change
resulted in confused and conflicting lines of authority and scarcities of
materials and labor. Tire manufacturing conformed to this general experience. Yet few industries attracted such debate or federal intervention; the
prospect of a debilitating rubber shortage threatened the war effort
throughout 1942 and 1943. The first response was rationing, and then,
amid indecision and argument, the federal government fundamentally
altered the industry's supply conditions by creating a synthetic rubber
industry.

Despite provision for federal stockpiling under the Strategic Materials Act, American stocks of rubber had declined to 125,000 long tons (lt)
during 1939. Buoyant demand and high rubber prices led manufacturers
to deplete their inventories further, but restocking began in 1940, and a
succession of German victories provoked slightly more earnest military
planning. A. L. Viles chaired a Rubber Industry Commission advising
the newly formed Council of National Defense. Management of the
federal stockpile was assigned to the Rubber Reserve Company (RRC),
part of the Reconstruction Finance Corporation (RFC). Imports in-

creased substantially, but the growing volume of civilian and military orders held stocks to 288,864 lt, perhaps 12 months supply, in 1940. By April 1941 the Office of Production Management (OPM) was advocating restraint by manufacturers; within two months fears of a rubber shortage induced stringent controls. RRC became the sole importer. The price of natural rubber was fixed at 22.5 cents per pound for the duration of the war. Corporate inventories were restricted, and firms were allocated rubber on the basis of their consumption in the year ending March 1941. Quotas were progressively tightened, with the production of white sidewall tires soon prohibited. Federal efforts to restrict automobile output, in order to conserve steel, encountered a poor response, but it did moderate OE demand. Smaller firms complained that OE suppliers could transfer their rubber quota between different markets. Tire manufacturing, thus, became one of the most extensively regulated sectors of American manufacturing well before Pearl Harbor. Rising demand, fixed rubber prices, and regulation provided a degree of stability, and there was less price discounting.

Mounting imports and domestic controls enabled rubber stocks to reach 500,000 lt when the U.S. entered the war in December 1941. In January 1942 the sweeping Japanese invasions of southeast Asia secured the principal rubber-producing regions, the source of 90 percent of American supplies. Once rubber in transit was delivered, the southeast Asian trade ceased completely, and the U.S. faced potential disaster. Wild rubber collection revived in South America in response to higher prices and subsidies. Firestone's Liberian plantations expanded production, and guayule, a rubber-bearing shrub grown in California, Arizona, and Texas, made a minor contribution. These alternative sources were poor compensation for the absent southeast Asian supplies. U.S. consumption of natural rubber was forced down from 376,791 lt to 105,429 lt, or by 72 percent between 1942 and 1945. This brutal contraction in the supply of a vital raw material triggered fragmented efforts to maintain defense needs.

On 11 December 1941 the manufacture and sale of new tires was prohibited, and the civilian market did not resume normal operations until New Year's Day 1946. No other item was subject to such lengthy rationing. Like all sectors, the industry experienced a disorganized and changeable mobilization. Military and civilian output was determined centrally by the War Production Board (WPB), although in practice the Armed Services established their own, often conflicting, priorities. Civilian demand was met, if at all, in an ad hoc fashion from remaining resources. OE production was limited indirectly by the automobile industry's conversion to munitions and the virtual abandonment of passenger car output. OE shipments declined from 19.8 million tires in 1941 to only 82,000 in 1943. Instead, tires were supplied for trucks, jeeps, aircraft, and other military equipment. Civilian bus and truck production was less restricted: total shipments increased from 11.6 million to 16.1 million units between 1941 and 1945. Given the bigger size of bus and truck tires, this expansion represented a substantially greater call on raw materials and plant capacity than would have been reflected in a similar increase in car tire production.

In 1941 nearly 30 million passenger cars were registered in the United States, and their existing tires were both the largest reserve of rubber and a potentially disastrous drain on current stocks. Following the ban on new tires sales, WPB fixed monthly rubber quotas for each type of tire, with a proportionate allocation for inner tubes. There was little civilian production during 1942 because military demand absorbed virtually all rubber supplies, although some tires were released from existing inventories. OPM subdivided the WPB quota among over 6,000 county and metropolitan tire rationing boards, which later assumed responsibility for other rationed commodities. Categories of eligible purchasers, primarily health and public safety workers plus certain bus and truck services, were designated, and local boards issued certificates authorizing new tire purchases. Worn tires had to be inspected by tire dealers who advised whether a replacement was warranted, and tire certificates could be refused if a driver was considered negligent in using tires.

Tire rationing boards commenced operations in January 1942, and civilian consumption and the categories of eligible purchasers were reduced steadily over the next 18 months. The industry shipped only 2.7 million new passenger car tires in 1942, which represented just 8 percent of the previous year's sales. OPA publicized car pooling, plant transportation schemes, and tire conservation. The resulting demand for used tires bid up prices swiftly until OPA imposed a price freeze in February 1942. Rationing was extended to recapped tires and tread rubber or "camelback," the unvulcanized compound used to retread a sound tire carcass. Manufacturers expanded camelback production: output rose from 75.9 million pounds to 339,718 million pounds between 1941 and 1944. Since effective recapping extended tire life, compulsory inspections were introduced for passenger tires during 1943 and 1944 and continued for truck tires until 1945.

Federal regulations limited the natural rubber content of each product and compelled manufacturers to turn to recycled rubber. RRC conducted a scrap rubber drive in the spring of 1942 and an "idle tire" campaign in the fall in a bid to obtain supplies for recycling. The destruction of old tires became illegal, and scrap rubber purchases continued throughout the war. By 1942 recycled rubber contributed 65 percent of total rubber consumption; it exceeded 80 percent in some months. Leading tire producers and independent reclaimers expanded output, and this proven recycling technology was a vital means of immediately extending existing supplies. The industry supplied 1.7 million "Victory" passenger tires composed entirely of recycled rubber in 1943. Yet greater output of recycled rubber only partially offset diminishing natural rubber supplies, and it was not a wholly satisfactory substitute. Tire performance deteriorated at high speeds and in large truck tires as the recycled rubber content increased.

Continuing mobilization pressed demand ever closer to current stocks, and growing fears of a shortage created internal conflicts over federal policies and priorities, which flared into bitter public disputes during 1942. In August congressional pressure compelled Roosevelt to appoint a Rubber Survey Committee, chaired by Bernard Baruch, to evaluate the whole rubber program. The Baruch committee recommended a new administrative appointment to coordinate policy, and in September 1942 William Jeffers took up the post of Rubber Director. Jeffers was succeeded a year later by his deputy, Bradley Dewey. The new office provided a louder voice in the clamor of wartime Washington since Jeffers endeavored to accelerate existing policies. Equally, the Rubber Director added to rather than reduced the diffusion of authority over different aspects of the rubber program. The principal departure proposed by the Baruch committee was the introduction of gasoline rationing and a 35 mph speed limit to reduce tire consumption even further.

Both Jeffers and the OPA favored tighter restrictions. Tire, automobile, and gasoline rationing were concentrated in OPA's Automotive Supply Rationing Division. In October 1942 the sale of used tires, the average consumer's only remaining legal source of supply, was prohibited as a preliminary to gasoline rationing. During the fall Jeffers and the OPA devised a system of monthly allocations of gasoline for each driver with the aim of achieving a national average of 5,000 miles per year. Essential services were assigning high mileage allowances; such drivers were often permitted better quality tires. Gasoline rationing was introduced in December 1942 and extended to overseas territories three months later. A local gasoline shortage had forced rationing in some northeastern states earlier in 1942, but the national scheme was based on the need to conserve tires rather than fuel.

Inevitably tire rationing presented difficulties. The original controls were modified to accommodate the particular needs of, for example, salesmen, migratory farm labor, ministers, and summer camp buses. As quotas contracted and the scope of rationing extended, even eligible purchasers could not be sure of obtaining tires during 1942 and 1943. Gasoline rationing had its greatest impact in southern states, where prewar mileages typically far exceeded the 5,000-mile average, but consumer and industry lobbying for higher regional allocations of gas was rejected. OPA instead preached the virtues of better tire conservation. The average driver was left to eke out existing tires. There was considerable scope for fraud and black market sales, particularly under gasoline rationing, which was difficult to police. OPA argued that tire rationing operated reasonably effectively without attracting undue public complaint given its pervasive impact. Certainly the measures substantially reduced civilian consumption by limiting total supply, and in this respect, they were crucial to the military buildup in 1942 and early 1943.

OPA recognized the threat that rationing posed to independent dealers and was anxious to preserve the existing distribution system. By prohibiting the delivery of previously ordered tires, OPA had compelled dealers to reimburse customers causing financial problems. This concern was articulated by dealers and manufacturers in congressional hearings during 1941 and 1942, which led to the passage of the Murray bill authorizing RFC assistance to retailers affected by rationing. OPA gave some relief through a tire return plan, allowing dealers to release excess tires to manufacturers. Firestone and Goodrich supplied other goods, including clothing, paint, and washing machines, to their dealers and stores. OPA restricted company outlets to their prewar proportions of each firm's sales to protect other retailers. Nonetheless, dealerships folded because of financial problems or their owners' entry into the armed services or more lucrative employment.

Rationing was relaxed in 1943, when 10.6 million replacement tires were shipped and output increased to 18.3 million in 1944. But production was still little more than half of 1941 sales, while the cumulative effects of tire wear and rationing constantly increased the volume of suppressed demand. WPB released more recycled rubber for passenger tires in late 1942, although this was offset by the freeze on used tire sales. During 1943 there was further easement, with passenger and truck tire recapping, used inner tubes, and truck camelback removed from the ration. In 1944 some factories were permitted to resume civilian production, and the construction of new plants was authorized. Yet civilian demand still received low priority, and the allied invasion of

Europe necessitated a renewed emphasis on military, especially truck tire, production in 1945.

☐ The Advent of Synthetic Rubber

Rationing, recycling, and tire conservation were accompanied by a search for substitutes for natural rubber. Manufacturers and federal officials first contemplated a synthetic rubber program in 1939, but there was little urgency before 1942. The rudimentary nature of the existing technology presented formidable technical, organizational, and political uncertainties. The challenge was to develop a compound, or elastomer, which would adequately reproduce the flexibility, durability, and processing qualities of natural rubber, and then to establish volume production. There had been some earlier work in this area. European scientists, notably Bourchardat (1879) and Tilden (1884), had used isoprene to create polymers possessing a chemical structure similar to natural rubber, and subsequent research identified butadiene as a more promising base. Record rubber prices stimulated further research between 1908 and 1910, but American interest diminished as plantation rubber drove down prices. The disruption to supplies during World War I stimulated rubber recycling in the U.S. rather than work on synthetics. However, German chemical firms faced more severe wartime shortages in World War I and undertook small-scale production of synthetic rubber, while the Russians devised a process for extracting butadiene from grain alcohol. Research activity was rekindled by higher rubber prices in 1925, and by 1933 I. G. Farben, the leading German chemical firm, had developed copolymers composed of butadiene and styrene (Buna-S). Further progress in Buna technology was delayed until the Nazi government encouraged the construction of two pilot plants in 1935 and 1936.

In 1930 I. G. Farben and Standard Oil (New Jersey) established a cooperative enterprise, the Joint American Study Company (JASCO), to exploit their various patents. The U.S. patents for Buna rubber were assigned to JASCO, and after 1937 Standard Oil produced butyl, a synthetic rubber that was highly impermeable to air and, thus, ideal for inner tubes. Other firms developed specialist synthetic rubbers, including Du Pont's chemical rubber Neoprene (1932), Goodyear's Chemigum (1927), and Goodrich's Koroseal (1926). The Thiokol Corporation introduced a rubber resin resistant to oil and gases in 1930. The specialist elastomers commanded premium prices and were superior to natural rubber for specific functions, such as insulation or fuel lines. However, production was small, and none were suitable, or intended, for tires.

Natural rubber prices, although volatile, were sufficiently low to deter investment in devising an all-purpose synthetic rubber. With Germany at war, the possibility of a seizure of U.S. patent rights led the partners to reorganize JASCO by dividing their spheres of influence. Standard Oil operated in the U.S. as well as the British and French empires, while I. G. Farben handled patent rights elsewhere. The new relationship gave Standard Oil control of the Buna-S patent, which offered the greatest potential for general use, but its advantage was devalued by Farben's tardy release of technical information during 1939 and 1940. Standard, ambitious for a leading role, offered Buna-S licenses to manufacturers, and Frank Howard, head of Standard's Research Division, hoped that an opening gambit of stringent royalty conditions would induce negotiations while full details of the process were being extracted from Farben. Howard envisaged a cooperative synthetic rubber venture with the leading tire companies in which Standard Oil traded the Buna patents for majority control.

Subsequently, the Department of Justice prosecuted Standard Oil for allegedly attempting to monopolize synthetic rubber production. Undoubtedly the company sought to maximize the returns from its rather uncertain grasp of Buna technology, but Howard's grand design underestimated the tire industry's traditional discord over patents. U.S. Rubber and Firestone sought Buna-S licenses, but Goodyear and Goodrich rejected the terms. In a defiant gesture Goodrich marketed the Ameripol tire containing 50 percent synthetic rubber in June 1940. Despite these early skirmishes, large-scale commercial production and use of synthetic rubber remained a remote prospect in 1940.

The commercial maneuverings acquired a strategic edge, albeit a dull one, from the stirrings of war preparedness. In 1939 tire firms and Standard Oil advocated federal support for synthetic rubber production. In June 1940 a Synthetic Rubber Committee, established to advise the Council of National Defense, recommended precautionary steps to establish 100,000 tons of capacity. These deliberations revealed serious financial, technical, engineering, and commercial uncertainties. The issue of federal financing gave the RFC a key role, but Jesse Jones, the agency's head, viewed the sketchy proposals unenthusiastically since he was optimistic about existing rubber stocks.

Between September 1940 and March 1941 the RFC, with Roosevelt's approval, shrank projected synthetic rubber capacity from 100,000 to 10,000 tons. Later William Knudsen from OPM intervened to ensure final agreement on a 40,000-ton program. The proposed synthetic rubber was designated GR-S (government rubber-styrene) and was to be based on the Buna-S mix of 75 percent butadiene and 25 percent styrene. The Defense Plant Corporation (DPC) contracted separately with Goodyear, Firestone, U.S. Rubber, and Hydrocarbon Chemical and Rubber, the last a joint venture between Goodrich and Phillips Petroleum. Each firm was to build and operate a 10,000-ton GR-S plant. Historians Herbert and Bisio emphasized the importance of technical advances in these early stages, but despite concern over rubber stocks, the expansion of synthetic rubber output from 8,383 lt to 22,434 lt during 1942 consisted largely of specialist, rather than all-purpose, synthetic rubbers.

Only the declaration of war imparted genuine urgency to the synthetic rubber program by ensuring a wholehearted commitment to federal financing of large-scale production. Planned capacity was raised from 40,000 tons to 400,000 in January 1942, 600,000 tons in March, and 800,000 tons a month later. Inconclusive discussions between Standard Oil, tire firms, and the RRC about patents and royalties were reconciled speedily in a cross-licensing agreement. In 1942 an antitrust suit resulted in a consent decree in which Standard Oil suspended royalty claims for the duration of the war. DPC financed additional GR-S plants, RRC met operating costs and regulated production, and the plants were run on a cost-plus fee basis by rubber companies. The distribution of GR-S capacity is shown in Table 7.1.

The four leading manufacturers were the principal agents, and each built and managed three GR-S facilities. General Tire was assigned a plant in Texas, and wider participation was achieved through two groups of lesser firms. Copolymer Corporation, which operated facilities in Baton Rouge, was a consortium of four tire companies (Armstrong, Dayton, Mansfield, and Pennsylvania) plus Sears, Roebuck, Armstrong's main customer. A Louisville plant was assigned to the National Synthetic Rubber Corporation, which consisted of Goodall Rubber, Hamilton Rubber, Hewitt, Lee Tire and Rubber, and the 3-M Company; Lee and 3-M's subsidiary, Inland, produced tires, while the other members were general rubber manufacturers. The federal government financed separate butadiene and styrene production facilities, operated by oil and chemical companies, to supply the essential materials for GR-S.

Between 1942 and 1945 federal expenditure on the synthetic rubber program totaled $673 million, and the new industry made a vital wartime contribution. GR-S production began in late 1942, although progress was handicapped by shortages of labor and construction materials, by changing forecasts of demand, which affected the priority given to synthetic rubber, and by the still experimental state of the technology. Full-capacity operations were not achieved until 1944, and there was recurring argument over the state of the program. In 1942 the farm lobby chal-

Table 7.1. Synthetic Rubber Capacity 1941–45

Firm	Plant Location	Capacity (lt)
Firestone	Akron, Ohio; Lake Charles, La.; Port Neches, Tex.	150,000
Goodyear	Akron, Ohio; Houston, Tex.; Los Angeles, Calif.	150,000
Goodrich	Louisville, Ky.; Borger, Tex.; Port Neches, Tex.	165,000
U.S. Rubber	Naugatuck, Conn.: Institute, W.V.; Los Angeles, Calif.	150,000
General Tire	Baytown, Tex.	30,000
Copolymer	Baton Rouge, La.	30,000
NSRC*	Louisville, Ky.	30,000
No. of Plants: 15		Total Capacity: 705,000

*National Synthetic Rubber Corporation

Source: Vernon Herbert and Attilro Bisio, *Synthetic Rubber: A Project That Had to Succeed*, (Greenwood Press, Westport, Conn.: 1985), 128, Table 11.2. © 1985 by Vernon Herbert and Attilro Bisio. Reprinted by permission.

lenged the emphasis on petroleum as the source of butadiene and championed grain alcohol as a supplementary source. Guy Gillette, an Iowa senator, organized congressional hearings to publicize this issue as well as broader criticisms of the rubber program. In July 1942 Congress authorized the creation of a rubber supply agency that would establish congressional direction of all rubber policies, but Roosevelt retained executive control by vetoing Gillette's bill. This political challenge forced the creation of the Baruch Committee to study federal rubber policies. The recommendations for a rubber director and gasoline rationing were noted earlier. On the issue of synthetic rubber production, the committee's report was broadly favorable, although alcohol-producing facilities were proposed for rural areas to counter the congressional pressure. The Baruch report defused the immediate controversy.

The episode aided the introduction of more stringent rationing by reemphasising the sense of crisis. There was even optimism as the GR-S plants came on stream. However, within a few months the questions of butadiene-from-alcohol had resurfaced. Butylene, the source of butadiene-from-petroleum, was also required for aviation fuel, and in early 1943 supplies appeared insufficient to meet both demands. With GR-S output lagging behind schedule, an intense intragovernment dispute over allocations of butylene revived the criticism of the RFC's emphasis on butadiene-from-petroleum. This finally led to large-scale investment in the alcohol process. Supplies of alcohol were released to the synthetic rubber program, existing butadiene from alcohol facilities at Institute, West Virginia and Kobuta, Pennsylvania, were extended, and a new plant was constructed at Louisville, Kentucky. Previously government and oil company officials had resisted the alcohol process in favor of butadiene from petroleum, which was cheaper, and thus, offered better long-term commercial prospects. However, the expensive alcohol method was a proven technology, which achieved full-scale operation swiftly, while the petroleum process was still in low gear. Butadiene-from-alcohol plants released butylene for aviation fuel and supplied 83 percent of the butadiene used in GR-S production during 1943. Without this contribution the synthetic rubber program would have been virtually ineffective in 1943. The 1943 butylene crisis was a damning indictment of earlier planning, especially following the Gillette bill and the Baruch Committee's report, but its resolution marked the first reversal of the rubber shortage. Production of synthetic rubber increased from 22,434 lt in 1942 to 773,673 lt in 1944, and GR-S accounted for 35 percent of rubber consumption in 1943 and 80 percent in the following year. The advent of a substitute for natural rubber increased supplies for the first time since 1941, although consumption remained below prewar levels and rationing was still necessary.

GR-S was priced at 50 cents per pound until April 1943, when full capacity operations allowed a reduction to 18.5 cents compared with a fixed natural rubber price of 22.5 cents. Higher prices were permitted in defense contracts, but the real cost of production was largely absorbed in basic federal funding of the synthetic rubber program. The increasing use of GR-S required adjustments in compounding, mixing, and vulcanization. For example, GR-S burned if mixed in the standard large batches, so firms had to install additional Banbury mixers, use a series of shorter mixes, and alter the GR-S compound. Product quality suffered because GR-S, like recycled rubber, performed poorly at the high temperatures generated by fast driving or within large tires.

The greater scale of U.S. mobilization and the halt to civilian output ensured that the war's impact far exceeded that of World War I. The major firms, as in other industries, dominated the shift into defense production. Output of mechanical goods, footwear, and vehicle and aircraft tires expanded, while new departments were created to produce gas masks, life jackets, rafts, pontoons, barrage balloons, and aircraft fuel tanks. Tire manufacturers followed the automobile industry into munitions production. U.S. Rubber established a Munitions Division to convert its Eau Claire, Wisconsin, tire plant and to operate six federal factories, including one producing explosives. Goodyear's Kelly-Springfield plant switched to the manufacture of shells and bullets, and Goodyear Engineering Corporation was created to run the government's Hoosier ordnance factory. Firestone's wartime activities included managing a U.S. arsenal.

The greatest departure from tire manufacturing was the involvement in aircraft manufacturing. An earlier interest in airships provided the basis for the Goodyear Aircraft Corporation (GAC), established in 1939 to supply airframes and components. GAC's workforce expanded from 1,320 in 1941 to 32,000 by 1944, when sales equaled Goodyear's rubber business. The company cooperated with automobile and aviation firms to produce bombers and fighter aircraft, and in 1941 DPC financed a new plant in Arizona. That same year the Firestone Aviation Products Company began supplying wheels, brakes, and other equipment. General Tire managed defense plants producing rockets and motors in Akron, California, and West Virginia, and converted its Indiana mechanical goods factory to manufacture military and aircraft supplies. General also purchased Aerojet, a missile manufacturer. Smaller firms generally depended on subcontracts and received more orders after 1943 as military demand pressed on capacity.

New defense plants were financed by DPC and operated by industrial corporations for management fees. Shortages of materials also encouraged innovations, particularly in compounding and the use of rayon rather than cotton in tire cord. Labor was the principal bottleneck. Tire industry employment increased from 57,500 to 102,500 between 1940 and 1945, shifts lengthened, and average hours worked weekly increased from 35.5 to 46.5 by 1944. Munitions and aircraft plants necessitated yet larger workforces; Goodrich alone employed 50,000 in 1945. Labor was transferred from tire production to other departments. The employment of women was vital in meeting demand, but labor turnover was persistently high, especially in Akron where aircraft plants, such as GAC, offered higher earnings. The resumption of civilian tire production in 1943 was hampered by labor shortages. Akron was designated a critical labor area and servicemen with experience of tire building were assigned to tire factories. Like other manufacturing industries, labor relations assumed a more formal style. Managers conceded union recognition in order to maintain production, and, with federal restrictions on wages, bargaining focused on working conditions and fringe benefits. URW

membership expanded and its organization and finances were strengthened, although wage controls limited its economic power. There were
frequent conflicts, notably a major strike in the Akron tire factories in
1943. Nevertheless, the war economy laid a firmer institutional base for
future industrial relations than had developed during the conflicts of the
1930s.

At the end of the war, defense contracts were canceled abruptly, and
manufacturers cautiously resumed civilian production. Gasoline rationing ceased on 15 August 1945, and OPA staged a gradual return to the
civilian tire market. The original system of tire certificates was re-
instated, and rationing continued until 1 January 1946. Meanwhile retailers were permitted to restock, and new tire dealers, especially war
veterans, were encouraged. Additional tire quotas were assigned to the
Mountain States when ex-servicemen driving east from Pacific ports
found their tires tending to blow out around Denver.

It is difficult to discern the full financial effects of the war on
manufacturing. Sales expanded and profits were good, but the picture is
complicated by wartime depreciation practices, management fees, federal investment, and price controls. The wartime stimulus to defense
production established a long-term involvement in aerospace, military,
and engineering activities. This shift had been foreshadowed by the
increasing interest in chemicals and mechanical goods during the 1930s
depression, but only wartime demand and conditions triggered major
diversification. More fundamentally, the federal synthetic rubber industry altered the tire industry's supply position by providing a new basic
raw material, although the fate of synthetic-rubber production and use
in peacetime was uncertain.

8

Reconversion, Synthetic Rubber, and Postwar Prosperity, 1945–1965

DURING THE FIRST POSTWAR DECADE, automobile sales expanded rapidly in response to pent-up demand and the introduction of new models. Consequently, OE sales increased from 1.1 million tires in 1945 to 11 million a year later (see Table 8.1), and OE demand, unchecked by the 1949 recession, totaled 42.5 million tires in 1955. This peak, however, was not surpassed for a decade; OE sales declined during the 1956, 1958, and 1960–61 recessions. The replacement sector displayed a different pattern. During 1946, replacement sales almost doubled to 54.6 million tires, and demand remained buoyant in 1947, but then declined over the next two years before reviving slowly. In the late 1950s the situation was reversed: buoyant replacement demand contrasted with poor OE sales.

In contrast to 1919 there were no new entrants after World War II. The number of manufacturers declined from 23 in 1945 to 17 by 1960. Memories of prewar competition discouraged new ventures as did the emphasis on OE business, which was beyond the reach of new firms. In 1947 the industry operated at full capacity and invested $55 million on new plant and equipment. Leading manufacturers purchased or leased defense plants that they had operated for the government: Goodyear acquired a plant in Kansas; Firestone leased facilities in Iowa and Pennsylvania; Goodrich purchased plants in Alabama and Oklahoma. Such immediate access to new capacity was a further discouragement to new market entrants. It also enabled the majors to accelerate their prewar

Table 8.1. Passenger Tire Industry, 1945–64

		Shipments (in thousands)		Shipment Index (1957 = 100)	
	Firms	OE	Replacement	OE	Replacement
1945	23	1,115	25,462	3	45
1946	22	11,086	54,684	34	97
1947	22	19,644	52,857	60	93
1952	18	24,106	45,458	74	80
1957	18	32,723	56,612	100	100
1962	16	37,461	78,430	115	139
1964	16	42,512	88,163	130	75

Source: Rubber Manufacturers' Association, *Rubber Industry Facts* 28, Table 26.

strategy of dispersing from Akron. The city accounted for 33 percent of tire capacity in 1947, only half of its 1930 share.

Shifting patterns of demand were reflected in the industry's structure. Concentration first increased slightly as Goodyear, Firestone, U.S. Rubber, and Goodrich benefited from the abnormally high level of OE demand; their combined business accounted for 79 percent of sales by 1954. Their share then fell to 70 percent in 1963 however, as replacement demand became the leading area. The main beneficiaries after 1955 were the fifth to ninth ranked firms whose combined market share increased from 13 percent to 19 percent between 1945 and 1963. Among the medium-size firms, General Tire, Mansfield, and Armstrong were most successful. In 1945 General Tire purchased around 45 percent of Mansfield's common stock and took full control of Pennsylvania Rubber. Four years later Pennsylvania's tire division was consolidated with Mansfield, while General Tire retained the sporting goods division. Mansfield obtained West Coast production and distribution by acquiring two Oakland firms. Inland Rubber, a subsidiary of the 3-M company, was purchased in 1950 and took a 50 percent holding in Pacific Tire and Rubber, which Mansfield extended to full control in 1960. In 1953 General Tire sold its Mansfield stock.

Declining replacement sales in the 1948 and 1949 recession undermined two small firms. Pharis abandoned automobile tire production. The Pharis trade name passed to Mansfield, but its bicycle tire business was transferred to Pharis's subsidiary, Carlisle. After two decades of financial strain, Norwalk Tire and Rubber's losses in 1947 and 1948 culminated in bankruptcy. The firm's plant was purchased by the neighboring Armstrong Rubber, whose growth continued to be based on its Sears's contract. Earlier Armstrong had absorbed Lake Shore Rubber, one of Sears's other suppliers.

☐ Sale of Federal Synthetic Rubber Industry, 1946–56

In 1946 the future of all-purpose synthetic rubber was uncertain. Butadiene-from-alcohol plants were closed; styrene plants were sold, and DuPont and Goodrich each purchased neoprene plants. The federal stockpile of natural rubber retained priority and determined the availability of natural rubber to manufacturers. Minimum levels of synthetic rubber consumption, always easily exceeded, remained in force to 1952, and government ownership of the synthetic rubber industry continued for a decade after the war. Firms still operated plants on a cost-plus fee basis. Federal funds financed $40.8 million of corporate and university research on synthetic technology through 1952.

During 1947 and 1948 there was a shift back toward natural rubber, which became cheaper than synthetic rubber. Synthetics were regarded as an inferior substitute. Industry and Congress opposed long-term government intervention, but commercial prospects were uncertain and strategic considerations demanded some assurance of adequate supplies. Smaller firms feared the major tire and oil companies' dominance of a private synthetic rubber industry, especially while mandatory use of synthetics continued. In the absence of any strategy, the 1948 Rubber Act renewed the existing program to June 1950 while recommending disposal of the plants. The return to natural rubber was checked in 1950. Output of synthetic rubber was already rising to accommodate domestic demand when in June the outbreak of the Korean War disrupted natural rubber imports. Federal controls were tightened. Manufacturers received supplies on the basis of their 1949–50 consumption, with maximum proportions of natural rubber specified for each product. When consumption exceeded formal targets, fears of a shortage prompted a more rigorous quota system after November 1950. The General Services Administration became the sole importer of rubber in December 1950. Several GR-S plants were reactivated, and the renewed crisis ensured a further extension of the Rubber Act, first to 1952 and then to 1954.

Civilian tire production was restricted in September 1950, and the National Production Authority progressively reduced allocations of rubber for replacement tires. Firms were required to produce more camelback for retreading as a conservation measure. The extreme stringency was relaxed in May 1951 as stockpiles accumulated and supplies of synthetic and recycled rubber increased. Remaining controls on consumption were lifted in the first quarter of 1952 after military demands eased, and the ending of import restrictions in July permitted a revival of passenger tire production.

The renewed disruption to the natural rubber trade between 1950 and 1952 firmly established synthetic rubber as the U.S. industry's primary raw material in contrast to the continuing reliance on natural rubber overseas. The volatility of natural rubber prices in 1950 was a salutary reminder of prewar episodes. Moreover, technological innovations were improving the quality of synthetics. Cold rubber, a prewar invention, was fully developed in 1947. By producing synthetic rubber at lower temperatures, a more durable compound resulted, which, once factory problems were overcome, was superior to the natural product for tire treads. The addition of oil or carbon black to the butadiene-styrene mix further improved the quality of synthetics and reduced their cost. Another advance was synthetic rubber, notably polyisoprene, that duplicated the chemical structure of natural rubber. Such innovations permitted wider use of synthetics.

The Rubber Producing Facilities Disposal Act of 1953 established a commission to conduct the sale of the synthetic rubber plants during 1955, subject to the approval of the Attorney General and Congress. Since 1948 synthetics' commercial prospects had improved markedly and offers were made for all facilities except the moth-balled Institute GR-S site and the butadiene-from-alcohol facilities. There was, however, competition for only 8 of the 27 plants, primarily those in California, which offered a degree of local market power. Following a period of negotiations, virtually all of the facilities were acquired by the same tire, oil, or chemical companies that had operated them. The sale realized $263 million with a further $140 million from equipment and inventories. General Tire's bid for the Baytown plant was rejected as too low, but it was sold a few months later; the Institute plant was sold in 1956. Goodyear and Firestone, both with two plants, were the leading producers of GR-S rubber. Goodrich and U.S. Rubber each acquired one plant and entered joint ventures with oil companies to obtain further plants. Goodrich and Gulf Oil formed Goodrich-Gulf Chemicals, and the Texas-U.S. Chemical Company was owned by U.S. Rubber and Texaco. The Copolymer consortium purchased the fully integrated Baton Rouge operations. Armstrong's stake increased steadily, and the firm became the sole owner of Copolymer in 1983. General Tire constructed its own facility in Odessa, Texas, in 1955.

In total, tire manufacturers accounted for three-quarters of GR-S output between 1955 and 1964. The integrated tire manufacturers consumed around 70 percent of their own synthetic rubber output and sold the remainder on the open market (see Table 8.2). Purchasers of government plants were obliged to supply a minimum proportion of their output to small business, and, with oil and chemical firms providing an independent source, supplies were readily available.

Table 8.2. Distribution of GR-S Rubber[1] Sales to Major Consuming Groups by Producer, 1962 (%)

Producer	Internal[2]	Affilates[3]	"Big 5"[4]	Other	Total
Goodyear	13.7		0.6	5.5	19.8
Firestone	12.0		0.2	4.6	16.8
Goodrich-Gulf		10.7	(x)	3.0	13.7
Texas-U.S.		7.8	(x)	1.9	9.7
Copolymer		6.2	0.3	2.4	8.9
Phillips			0.3	6.0	6.3
Shell			2.6	2.9	5.5
American Synthetic Rubber Company		2.5	0.7	3.1	6.3
United Rubber			0.4	4.2	4.6
General	3.8		0.7	1.3	5.8
U.S. Rubber	0.5		0.3	1.2	1.7
Other[5]	0.1			0.8	0.9

1. By 1962 GR-S rubber was known as S-type or SBR.

2. Transfers to manufacturing plants owned by the same firm.

3. Related firms such as Goodrich in the case of Goodrich-Gulf.

4. Goodyear, Firestone, Goodrich, U.S. Rubber, and General Tire.

5. Dewey and Almy Chemical, W.R. Grace, and International Latex.

(x) = sales totaling < 0.1 percent

Source: *Eighth Report of the Attorney-General on Competition in the Synthetic Rubber Industry*, 13.

Between 1952 and 1955 the government held the basic price of GR-S at 23 cents per pound, plus a fixed rate for freight costs. The standard price remained constant for six years following the transfer to private ownership. New types of synthetic rubber were more expensive, but prices nonetheless fell in real terms and discounting began. The U.S. attorney general noted the fixed GR-S prices with concern, but concluded that the synthetic rubber industry was competitive. Improved synthetic rubber quality and technical services for the customer, such as advice on compounding, were the principal forms of competition, as noted by historian Charles Phillips. Development of synthetic rubber production was a significant break with the earlier dependence on imported natural rubber. Synthetic rubber producers varied output and inventories, rather than price, in response to demand. Thus, tire manufacturers' synthetic rubber subsidiaries incurred sizable inventory and fixed costs in return for the degree of independence from the still volatile natural rubber market. With synthetics providing 60 percent of all new rubber and the ability to select between synthetics, natural, and recycled rubber, the industry achieved a measure of cost stability that it had desired since the 1910s. The impact of synthetics on costs was greater for other rubber products because vehicle tires required a higher proportion of natural rubber; truck and bus tires were still made entirely of natural rubber.

☐ Changing Tire Design, 1945–1964

Tire casings had been constructed from plies of cotton cord and rubber, but wartime advances provided synthetic fibers that were lighter, more resilient, and less expensive. Rayon cord was employed on a small scale after 1936 and performed better than cotton at the higher running temperatures of tires containing synthetic rubber. Rayon accounted for 46 percent of tire fabrics in 1946 and had superseded cotton by 1954. Nylon cord was used after 1942, but stretched so much that tires on parked cars appeared flat. Although these "flat spots" disappeared as the car was driven, they produced an initial thumping sound and an odd appearance. However, new and cheaper types of nylon resulted in nylon tire cord exceeding rayon use in 1963. Each new product was accompanied by considerable marketing effort, often by fiber suppliers, stressing safety and durability. A major innovation was the tubeless tire, patented in 1928 and produced commercially by Goodrich in 1948. The inner tube was replaced by a thin lining that sealed air inside the casing providing an airtight fit. By

1954–55 tubeless tires accounted for virtually all OE sales. General consumer acceptance was slower, but by 1960 tubeless tires supplied two-thirds of the replacement market.

Manufacturers also experimented with wire or steel cord. Michelin had marketed wire cord tires for off-the-road vehicles in the U.S. in the late 1930s and in 1948 patented the radial tire. During the war U.S. Rubber investigated wire cord for the government, and several firms studied the idea in the mid-1940s. However, wire cords tended to break at the prevailing low tire pressures and were more expensive than rayon, thus American firms concentrated on synthetic fibers. Michelin's expertise in steel radial tires was to emerge as a major factor in the 1970s.

The new synthetic materials and changing tire designs illustrate the increasingly scientific nature of tire manufacturing. They were also a continual challenge to factory operations. Rayon cord was liable to become deformed during the building and curing processes, while nylon required smaller molds. Tubeless tires took longer to assemble, but eliminated inner tube production. Productivity continued to improve, but product changes restricted volume production. With innovations usually spreading from the OE sector, larger manufacturers incurred the initial development costs, but they gained as new products came into wider use. Smaller firms had to follow the innovations or face a declining market for older style tires.

□ Tire Markets: Trends and Competition

The handful of new automobile producers in the 1940s made little market impact, and the number of independents was reduced by mergers in the 1950s. A pattern of business relations was evident in the OE sector. U.S. Rubber was General Motors's largest supplier and retained its position even when an antitrust suit forced DuPont to dispose of its General Motors's stock in the 1960s. Firestone had the largest share of Ford's orders, and Goodyear dominated sales to Chrysler and American Motors. Both General Motors and Ford also assigned contracts to firms other than their principal suppliers.

General Tire's entry into the OE market in 1955 added to the car firms' bargaining power. Profit margins remained relatively low, but the leading firms benefited from the unusual strength of OE sales; by 1955 production was at record levels—7.9 million cars and 42.5 million tires. At this point OE orders accounted for 45 percent of total demand compared with a prewar average of 29 percent. But the percentage soon dropped back to prewar levels, and it was a decade before sales surpassed 1955 levels.

In the postwar replacement market, manufacturers initially supplied only the profitable first-line tires, but normal conditions soon reappeared. Western Auto Supply and Sears reduced first-line prices in 1946 in response to lost market share. Manufacturers, while formally retaining list prices, sanctioned discounts, and second-line tires were adopted widely when replacement orders declined in 1948. The 1949 recession prompted further rebating, discounting, and extended warranties. Major firms had the cushion of rising OE demand, but smaller firms faced greater pressure as margins narrowed. In 1949 Penfield Seiberling noted ruefully that "it is really beginning to seem like old times." However, the recession was mild, replacement sales revived in the second half of the year, and a group of medium and small producers agitated successfully for higher prices. Korean War controls reduced replacement sales sharply in 1951 and limited the range of tires permitted. Relaxation of the controls was followed by a sustained rise in replacement sales from 45.4 million tires in 1952 to 68.4 million in 1960, and 78.4 million two years later (see Table 8.1). Sales expansion was one consequence of a further increase in motoring. Postwar economic growth was accompanied by wider car ownership, and the suburbanization of American cities made the car more important in commuting to work. Motoring was also a major element in higher spending on recreation and leisure activities. Long-distance driving was promoted by the new road-building programs by states and then by the federal government with the 1956 Interstate Highway Act. The federal program was financed in part by a tax on tires and inner tubes.

Tire dealers still accounted for around half of replacement sales in 1946, but their share drifted down over the next two decades (see Table 8.3). A few companies relied almost entirely on this outlet. McCreary Tire and Rubber distributed only first-line tires through some 800 dealers in 1962, with the bulk of sales made within 500 miles of its Pennsylvania plant.

Tire, Battery, and Accessory (TBA) sales to oil companies provided one quarter of replacement tire sales during the 1950s. In 1951 Atlantic Refining switched suppliers from Lee to Goodyear and Firestone to ensure improved distribution. The manufacturers canvassed Atlantic's franchised service stations, and the oil company received a commission on sales. Such commission or "override" contracts gave the wholesale function to the tire firm, but following complaints, the Federal Trade Commission concluded that the arrangements restrained trade because service station operators felt coerced into buying from certain suppliers. The FTC's decision, upheld by the Supreme Court, ensured that oil

Table 8.3. Distribution of Replacement Tire Sales, 1946–64 (%)

Year	Independent Dealers	Mail-Order Chain Stores	Company Stores	Department Stores	Oil Companies
1946	52.2	17.0	9.6	2.5	18.7
1948	48.9	16.1	7.5	3.0	24.5
1953	43.6	19.8	8.7	3.0	24.9
1957	44.2	18.2	8.2	2.8	26.6
1961	41.2	20.2	9.2	4.4	24.9
1964	38.8	22.4	10.3	5.0	23.5

Source: Federal Trade Commission, *Economic Report on the Manufacture and Distribution of Automotive Tires.* appendix table 18.

companies continued acting as wholesalers to service stations rather than involving producers directly. Nonetheless, the four leading tire firms dominated TBA business.

Middling firms took the largest share of mail-order and chain store contracts. Armstrong secured the greatest stability by maintaining its close links with Sears. Small manufacturers, such as Lee and Dayton, expanded their private brand business in the 1950s. Cooper Tire and Rubber established its own national wholesaling system between 1947 and 1964, which strengthened its ability to supply private brand customers. Even Seiberling obtained its first private brand contract in 1953.

The most aggressive sales policies were conducted by Mohawk and Mansfield. Mohawk opened 14 warehouses between 1949 and 1960 to supply customers. Mansfield's acquisitions of the Pennsylvania, Inland, and Pacific plants as well as the Pharis trademark consolidated its position in the low-price end of the market. In 1958 Mansfield contracted with Montgomery Ward and a year later opened a factory in Mississippi. The strategy depended on low prices, narrow margins, and new low-cost plants. The risk of a major customer switching suppliers increased, however, as more firms pursued the same marketing policy. The loss of a major contract weakened Mansfield's financial position in 1960.

Independent retailers innovated by selling their own brand tires using leased space in department stores. This sector expanded from 0.2 percent to 1.8 percent of replacement sales between 1947 and 1960. The Abel Corporation's 46 outlets accounted for one-third of leased store sales by 1961. The other pioneers were Vanderbilt Tire and Rubber (later VTR) with 44 outlets and American Auto Stores. In effect these enterprises maintained the trend toward multiple outlets and private brands while providing a variant on the role of the chain stores.

Changing tire designs produced a yet more complex pricing structure in the replacement market. Rayon, nylon, and later polyester cord tires provided the opportunity to seek premium prices. Manufacturers also sought to differentiate tires in terms of function, style, and consumer taste. White sidewall tires were reintroduced after the Korean War. They provided a form of product differentiation that was well suited to the automobile industry's mania for styling in the 1950s. The width of the white stripe could be varied, and later firms used white lettering as a feature. Firms successfully promoted specialist mud and snow tires, using expertise in tread design and rubber compounding to promote additional tire purchases. Such strategies were the reverse of the private brand business, which emphasized price.

The cumulative effect of changing tire designs was a proliferation of tire lines and prices. Seiberling Rubber manufactured 67 lines of passenger tires in 1951, and 87 lines in 1955, plus an additional 27 Atlas lines for Standard Oil. By 1961 Seiberling's range had expanded to an extraordinary 280 of its own brands plus 42 Atlas lines. Pricing was further complicated by a variety of discounts. The Federal Trade Commission identified a shift toward second- and third-line tires. In 1953 premium and first lines accounted for 85 percent of replacement sales, but their share had declined to 60 percent in 1955 and 40 percent by 1959. Meanwhile the proportion of second lines increased from 15 percent to 45 percent. The share of third-line tires rose from nil in 1953 to 15 percent six years later. Initially this was a readjustment after the industry's abnormal ability to rely on first-line tires following World War II and the Korean War. Despite a downward drift, tire industry profits were excellent in the 1950s. However, as OE sales became sluggish, leading firms reacted to the success of smaller producers in the replacement sector, and a series of developments culminated in the most intense price competition since the 1930s.

☐ Competition and Acquisition, 1958–1965

In 1958 Firestone obtained its first private brand business, adding a new element to the low-price sector and the leading firms' rivalries. Then U.S. Rubber revived the stores program abandoned two decades earlier and by 1961 had 166 stores. Goodrich, Goodyear, and General Tire also extended their retailing activities. The overall growth of company stores is summarized in Table 8.4.

Table 8.4. Number of Manufacturer-Owned Stores among the Five Leading
Tire Firms, 1955–61

	1955	1957	1961
Goodyear	491	539	699
Firestone	722	759	784
Goodrich	499	507	604
U.S. Rubber	0	1	166
General	72	107	164
Other Firms	n.a.	n.a.	36

Source: U.S. Senate, Committee on Small Business, *Studies in Dual Distribution*,
7.

Between 1959 and 1964 company stores increased their share of the replacement market from 7.8 percent to 10.3 percent, yet the principal gains accrued to General Tire and Mansfield. U.S. Rubber's return to retailing apparently intensified competition among the industry leaders rather than immediately weakening lesser firms.

Competition received a decisive twist when Goodyear announced price reductions of between 5 percent and 19 percent on premium and first-line tires in August 1959. Goodyear described the move as counterinflationary. Managerial changes may also have been a factor. In 1958 Russell De Young was appointed as Goodyear's new president, and Victor Holt, Jr. took executive control of sales. Similar management changes at U.S. Rubber and Goodrich brought a new emphasis on marketing. A 1966 Federal Trade Commission report suggested that Goodyear was seeking to improve its first-line sales and simultaneously counter charges of price fixing against the industry.

In June 1959 a Federal Trade Commission complaint against the Rubber Manufacturers' Association and fifteen producers alleged agreements on list prices and discounting. The complaint claimed that the cooperative strategies of the 1930s were revived after World War II with firms exchanging price lists, coordinating discount policies and price changes, and using the RMA's 1933 cost accounting formula. After initial hearings the RMA and other defendants accepted a consent decree in which they agreed to "cease and desist" without admitting the charges. In the absence of archival material it is difficult to evaluate the degree of cooperation in the 1950s.

The FTC's evidence on pricing referred primarily to the period between 1946 and 1956, when the major producers' market share was rising. Firms and trade associations continued the 1930s debates over prices and trade practices. Conceivably the FTC's interest checked such discussions and contributed to renewed price competition in 1959. At the same time the lack of cooperation in the 1930s suggests that any agreements were likely to weaken with the decline in OE orders after 1955.

Prices had been declining after 1957, but Goodyear's price reductions pushed the wholesale price index back to its 1950 level. Since the index applied only to list prices of first-line tires, it did not reflect current discounting or the prices of lower-quality tires. Goodyear's decision, in fact, represented a substantial narrowing of differentials between first-line and other prices. There was no general price increase until March 1962. List prices were constant in 1960, but discounting pushed actual prices still lower and all firms placed greater emphasis on third lines. The result, as it was three decades earlier, was financial pressure, especially on medium-size producers whose average profits fell below those of the industry leaders between 1960 and 1965.

In 1961 the U.S. economy embarked on an impressive upswing. Automobile sales and OE demand rose strongly until 1965, and replacement sales began recovering in 1962. A notable development was the establishment of modern tire plants in the South and Midwest between 1959 and 1968. A series of acquisitions in marketing and production contributed to the industry's vigor. U.S. Rubber bought several regional wholesale chains, and Goodyear's Kelly-Springfield subsidiary purchased a Texas wholesaler. Department store leasing offered an attractive growth area, and in 1961 Mansfield boldly acquired the Abel Corporation and quadrupled Abel's outlets. Mansfield also absorbed a Boston company. This acquisition strategy contributed significantly to the medium-size firms' expanding share of company store sales.

Goodrich established car care centers in department stores as well as purchasing Vanderbilt Tire and Rubber (VTR) and doubling its leased outlets. Kelly-Springfield acquired American Auto Stores in 1963. New outlets and additional marketing effort raised the department store sector from 1.8 percent to 5 percent of replacement sales between 1960 and 1964 and altered the business from overwhelmingly private brands to the manufacturers' own second and third lines. Goodyear and Firestone seized the leadership of the acquisition movement. In 1965 Goodrich sold its Vanderbilt chain back to VTR, which immediately resold it to Goodyear for $10 million. Firestone paid $6 million for Mansfield's Abel outlets.

Despite lower prices the major producers suffered a slight loss of market share between 1958 and 1961. The principal beneficiaries were aggressive firms such as Mansfield, Mohawk, and Armstrong. Other small firms were weakened financially. Schenuit Rubber abandoned passenger tire production in 1959. Three independent producers were absorbed by major firms. Firestone acquired Dayton's tire division in 1961 and Seiberling's tire division in 1964. After closure during a two-year strike, Lee's tire operations were purchased by Goodyear in 1965. Mansfield, the most ambitious of the middling producers in its marketing and acquisitions, sold its tire distribution system to Firestone in 1965, but retained tire production, including a 10-year contract to supply Firestone on a cost-plus basis in return for technical assistance. The acquisitions strengthened Firestone's and Goodyear's ability to promote product differentiation and to compete with cheaper tires without debasing their own brand names.

After 1961 the combined effects of price competition, renewed OE demand, and the acquisition policy enabled the leading manufacturers to regain market share. Among the smaller firms, however, there was no simple formula for survival and no single cause of failure. Postwar swings in output and the need to keep abreast of changing tire designs created difficulties for small producers. Seiberling had relied on independent tire dealers, and its prices were close to the major firms' first lines. Goodyear's 1959 reduction of price differentials effectively squeezed Seiberling from above; meanwhile, the firm could not match the costs and prices of smaller manufacturers or private brands. Seiberling distributed nationally, but it was a high-cost producer compared with new tire plants with longer shifts and modern facilities.

Seiberling did obtain a private brand contract with Standard Oil and established a new industrial plastics factory that produced rigid PVC (polyvinyl chloride). However, the new investments absorbed considerable cash; earnings and dividends remained poor. In August 1955 Edward Lamb, a Toledo businessman, began buying Seiberling stock. Both Penfield Seiberling and Lamb advocated diversification, but a dispute over the composition of the board signaled an acrimonious struggle for control, which simmered between 1956 and 1959. Eventually competitive pressures in the early 1960s swung the conflict against the existing management. Seiberling's financial position deteriorated with an overall loss, the first since 1949, of $1.4 million in 1961. In August 1961 Penfield Seiberling relinquished executive power in favor of Harry Schrank, the factory manager. Seiberling, who remained chairman, hoped that the move would moderate Lamb's criticisms of the Seiberling family while maintaining control by the existing management, but it proved a fatal misjudgment. By March 1962 Edward Lamb had majority control, Schrank had allied himself with Lamb, and Penfield Seiberling had resigned as chairman. The new management reorganized financial and management systems and personnel and continued the efforts to develop private brand sales and to diversify.

Nonetheless, Seiberling recorded a record deficit in 1964. Short-term borrowing totaled $11.5 million, and the tire division was losing around $400,000 a month. Seiberling's Canadian operation, also in difficulties, was sold to Goodyear's Canadian subsidiary. Seiberling's U.S. tire operations were finally purchased by Firestone in 1964. Harry Schrank became president of the Seiberling division of Firestone until his retirement in 1967; the plant was modernized after its acquisition by Firestone.

Seiberling's decline was brought about by its lack of diversification, private brand contracts, and low-cost tire plants. Yet even these elements were not always sufficient protection against the intense competition following the narrowing of price differentials in the early 1960s. Cooper possessed private brand and low-price tire business, but still operated at a loss in 1960. Dayton was more diversified than Seiberling, while Lee and Mansfield possesed sizable private brand business, but all experienced financial problems. Financial constraints impeded diversification at Seiberling. With Mansfield financial problems were the result of expansion and emphasized the difficulty of breaking into mass distribution.

As in other industries, smaller manufacturers sought more profitable sectors in which mass production and distribution were less influential. Truck tires provided higher value per unit and were less subject to capital-intensive production. Local distribution and retreading services could provide good business opportunities. Truck tire sales were weak between 1952 and 1957, but expanding demand in the early 1960s was an attractive alternative to increasingly competitive passenger tire markets. By 1962 truck tires accounted for 45 percent of McCreary's sales compared with 24 percent from car tires. Schenuit Rubber concentrated on aircraft and industrial tires, and Carlisle specialized in bicycle, motorcycle, and small industrial tires. Major firms were less dominant in such sectors: the nine leading companies accounted for 54 percent of tractor and industrial tire sales compared with their 92 percent share of the passenger tire market.

□ Diversification

Depression in the 1930s and war in the 1940s had promoted diversification in order to reduce dependence on tires, exploit new research, and respond to wartime demands. Successful wartime investments were often retained and expanded during the Korean War. Goodyear Aircraft

Corporation (GAC) purchased an Arizona plant in 1949 and supplied a diverse range of products, including airships, airframes and components, fuel tanks, and steel products, as well as developing missile and space-related business. GAC employed 3,500 before the Korean War and 8,500 in the late 1950s. General Tire's Aerojet-General subsidiary manufactured rockets and rocket motors; an industrial products division produced metal and plastic components for aircraft and electrical goods. Firestone concentrated on its automotive products business begun in the 1930s, and firms of all sizes expanded their mechanical and industrial goods divisions. DayCo, formerly Dayton Rubber, relied on this business following the sale of its tire operations. Carlisle used a series of acquisitions to enter the production of machinery, wire, and electrical goods. Goodrich and U.S. Rubber expanded their established expertise in the chemical industry. This field, strengthened by involvement in synthetic rubber, was important for many firms. All firms were interested in the developing plastics industry, which provided a substitute for some rubber products and scope for applying existing skills in a related sector. Advances in rubber chemistry were part of a rapid development of polymer technology. There were costs and uncertainties in entering new spheres, and the plastics industry was very competitive because of the number of new entrants.

There were more eclectic forms of diversification. Goodyear Atomic Corporation, a new subsidiary, contracted with the Atomic Energy Commission to operate an Ohio plant producing uranium isotopes in 1954. In 1956 General Tire acquired a majority interest in A. M. Byers, a wrought-iron and steel pipe manufacturer, and accumulated major holdings in the radio, television, and film industries. During the 1930s Bill O'Neil, eldest son of the firm's founder, had invested in local radio stations; in 1942 General purchased the Yankee network in New England. Another son, Tom, expanded these interests through a series of acquisitions, including RKO Pictures in 1955. The movie side was sold in 1958, but the RKO-General subsidiary continued in radio and television.

9

Radials, Recession, and Reorganization, 1970–1989

BETWEEN 1965 AND 1969 TIRE SALES GREW by 3.6 percent per annum, only half the rate during the previous five years. Tire markets were diverging. Original equipment sales declined by 2.2 percent, while replacement sales increased by 6.4 percent, maintaining the earlier emphasis on the replacement sector. Demand then contracted when a General Motors's strike coincided with the trough of the 1969–70 recession. Soon thereafter, tire sales, shadowing automobile output, recovered strongly to a record total of 201.6 million units in 1973. In retrospect, it was the end of an era. Unit sales did not regain their 1973 levels for 11 difficult years as both OE and replacement demand steadily fell. Sales declined at an annual average rate of 4.7 percent between 1973 and 1980, and U.S. manufacturers proved poorly equipped for profound changes in their product and industry.

☐ The Advent of Radial Tires

After 1941 tires assumed a wider, flatter shape; manufacturers introduced synthetic rubbers and fabrics and tubeless tires. Yet the basic structure of the tire altered little. The tire carcass was built up from plies of rubberized fabric and finished with a patterned rubber tread. Since the early 1900s the carcass has been constructed on a bias principle in which cords within the fabric were arranged at an angle of between 25 and 40 degrees to the direction traveled. In 1968 92 percent of U.S. output was of bias tires. There was, however, an alternative radial construction in which the cords were placed at 90 degrees to the direction traveled. The radial concept was invented in 1913, but its first practical application was by Michelin in France in 1948. Michelin also placed a steel belt between the plies of rubberized fabric and the rubber tread; the Pirelli firm later devised a rayon belt.

Radial construction offered dramatic advantages. The belt diminished the twisting effect of contact with the road and the firmer carcass lowered the internal temperature of the tire when in motion. The result was improved wear; a radial tire averaged 40,000 miles compared with around 23,000 miles for a bias tire in 1970. Handling improved, and, because radials generated less internal friction, so did fuel consumption. There were disadvantages. Radials provided less cushioning and, like balloon tires in the 1920s, were incompatible with existing vehicle suspensions and could not be mixed with bias tires. Radials were also more complex and time-consuming to assemble. Nonetheless, by the early 1960s Michelin, Pirelli, and other European firms were expanding radial sales.

Although their European subsidiaries experimented with the new tire, American producers lagged. Goodrich proclaimed their merits from 1964, but failed to stimulate OE orders, while Goodyear and Firestone announced radial lines, but were cautious about the new design. The industry was uncertain whether Detroit would forsake the traditional soft ride of American automobiles since the 1920s. Manufacturers were reluctant to incur the substantial costs of scrapping bias capacity and financing a full-scale conversion to radials, which required far more expensive machinery.

The U.S. industry finally compromised by introducing the bias-belted tire, which retained the bias principle of angled cords, but incorporated a belt underneath the tread. Bias-belted tires were broadly consistent with established factory operations. Their longer life commanded higher prices; bias-belted tires averaged 30,000 miles, which placed them midway between bias and radial tires in terms of durability. Bias-belted tires accounted for 87 percent of OE sales by 1970 and 58 percent of the replacement market two years later. Manufacturers constructed new plants, and the transition saw polyester displacing nylon as the principal tire fabric. Bias-belted tires proved lucrative and U.S. firms assumed that radials would be adopted slowly on more expensive cars. Ford in 1970 and General Motors in 1972 announced plans to fit steel-belted radials on some models. Suddenly expectations were confounded by dramatic external changes, and the switch to radials had to be undertaken swiftly in adverse conditions. In part, tire firms were too indecisive, and, in part, they suffered from Detroit's complacency over product quality.

In October 1973 the Yom Kippur War led to output restrictions imposed by the Organization of Petroleum Exporting Countries (OPEC) and an embargo on oil exports to nations sympathetic to Israel. Gasoline prices rose 35 percent during 1974, and American motorists experienced rationing and lines at gas stations. Radials' contribution to improved fuel efficiency now assumed greater significance, and car producers accelerated introduction of the tire abruptly. Radials' share of OE sales leaped from 5 percent in 1972 to 41 percent two years later and 61 percent by 1975 (see Table 9.1). The replacement sector changed more gradually, but radials accounted for 24 percent of sales in 1975 and forged ahead thereafter. The momentum was maintained when the Iranian revolution restricted oil supplies and further increased fuel prices in 1979–80. Radials had taken over the OE market by 1981 and continued to penetrate the replacement sector.

The sudden adoption of radials was complicated by cyclical factors. The economy entered a severe recession in the final quarter of 1973; OE sales contracted by 23 percent in 1974 and fell further in the following year as car sales declined. The tire industry operated at only 68 percent of capacity in 1975. In 1976 automobile output recovered strongly, and

Table 9.1. Passenger Tire Construction by Sector, 1971–87 (%)

	OE			Replacement		
	Bias	Belted-Bias	Radial	Bias	Belted-Bias	Radial
1971	13	85	2	49	45	6
1973	18	64	18	45	42	13
1975	9	30	61	38	38	24
1977	10	22	68	36	26	38
1979	15	9	76	33	19	48
1981	0	1	99	25	16	59
1983	0	0	100	17	13	70
1985	0	0	100	9	10	81
1987	0	0	100	3	6	91

Source: *Modern Tire Dealer*, "Annual Facts Directory," January 1972, 46; January 1974, 54; January 1980, 26; January 1982, 46; January 1987, 37; January 1988, 37.

rising OE and, with a slight lag, replacement demand brought total tire sales to 193.9 million by 1978, close to 1972 levels. However, the second oil crisis imposed a further check: tire sales slumped from 174 million to 146 million between 1979 and 1980. The impact of recessions on OE demand was aggravated by simultaneous changes in the variables affecting replacement sales. During the 1973 oil embargo, the U.S. speed limit was reduced from 65 mph to 55 mph in order to conserve fuel, and the lower level remained in force after the embargo ended in mid-1974. Average vehicle speed declined from 65 mph in 1973 to 57.6 mph in 1974, reducing tire wear. Higher fuel prices, lower speeds, and the radials' longer life all reduced replacement demand.

In this unfavorable and shifting environment, manufacturers had to establish expensive new capacity for a radial technology in which they lacked expertise. Average plant size increased sharply, and volume and economies of scale assumed greater significance. Radials required new tire-building machinery and molds as well as modifications to the vulcanization process. The use of steel wire in the belt presented technical problems and placed a premium on quality control. Productivity growth slowed, and with demand and profits declining, the new investment increased indebtedness and financial pressures. There were further difficulties. The 1973–74 oil crisis imparted an added upward twist to synthetic rubber prices: Goodrich's raw material costs reportedly increased 51 percent in the twelve months to September 1974. In August 1971 the Nixon administration imposed a 90-day freeze on wages and prices followed by a second phase after November during which price increases required prior approval from the Cost of Living Council. A second freeze was imposed in June, and general controls were not finally abolished until April 1974. The price controls assumed constant productivity growth, but tire manufacturers complained that their switch to radials impeded efficiency and prevented the industry from recouping its costs. During phase two, however, firms were unable to implement a permitted increase fully due to a sluggish market; demand rather than price control provided the constraint.

Table 9.2 traces the industry's retrenchment in the face of the formidable impact of radials, higher oil prices, and cyclical influences. Output, capacity, and employment declined in the industry's most extensive reorganization since the 1930s. The brunt of the contraction fell on bias and bias-belted plants. New radial facilities were concentrated in the Midwest and South. Akron retained corporate headquarters and research facilities, but the "Rubber City's" loss of tire manufacturing, which had begun between 1926 and 1945, was completed. Passenger tire production in Akron ended in 1978; truck tire production left in 1983–

Table 9.2. Trends in the Passenger Tire Industry, 1973–87

	Firms	Plants	Factory Employment	Output (millions)	Index of Output (1978 = 100)
1973	12	n.a.	88,300	201.6	104
1978	14	52	81,000	193.9	100
1983	11	35	52,200	182.0	94
1987	12	32	n.a.	202.7	105

Sources: Firms and plants derived from *Modern Tire Dealer* "Annual Facts Directory," January 1978, 75–76; January 1983, 53–54; January 1988, 48–49. Output and employment from *Statistical Abstract of the United States,* 1975, 357; 1979, 412, 647; 1985, 413; 1987, 584.

84; in 1987 Goodrich's aircraft tire operation was relocated. The majors' withdrawal left only small firms manufacturing in Ohio. Firms also withdrew from the West Coast, and by 1980 only Armstrong possessed a California factory. Production was now centered in Alabama, Oklahoma, and the Carolinas, where companies sought lower wages and taxes and had a few nonunion plants.

The leading firms attempted to reduce debt through plant closures and layoffs. Historian Charles Jeszeck identified changing industrial relations policies in the tire industry after 1967 ("Structural Change in CB," *Industrial Relations,* 1986, 229–47). In the postwar period the URW established a strong bargaining position and succeeded in organizing many of the new tire plants. The union established national agreements and pursued a strategy of targeting one firm for a strike and applying the terms of the eventual settlement throughout the industry. In 1967, however, the five major manufacturers agreed on a Mutual Assistance Pact with the intention of reducing the impact of strikes against individual firms. In the early 1970s management had some success in limiting wage increases. The union, in turn, was more assertive after rising inflation eroded real earnings in the mid-1970s. Management conceded higher wages after a 144-day strike in 1976 but increasingly sought local agreements and changes to working practices. After 1979 contraction of capacity and the financial problems of the firms weakened the union's position and led to major changes in working practices. By the 1980s the industry had moved to eight-hour shifts and continuous operation. Workers in many older plants made concessions to individual firms (notably General and Goodrich) in a bid, usually unsuccessful, to avoid closures. Unions made few inroads into the new radial plants, and the new multinational firms who entered the U.S. market also introduced different work practices.

Goodyear proved a durable industry leader. Despite closing bias factories, it recovered from tentative beginnings with radials by investing some $1.5 billion on new capacity in the late 1970s and, thus, retained a dominant position. Goodyear was the most profitable of the leading firms. Its Kelly-Springfield and Lee subsidiaries supplied second-line or associate brands, which strengthened Goodyear's presence in the low-price sector. After the Lee plant closed in 1980, Lee then marketed tires made in other Goodyear factories. Firestone remained in second place, but its tire division was unprofitable from 1978 to 1980. The recall of the Firestone "500" radial in 1978 undermined the confidence and resources necessary for new investments. Firestone decided against a merger with Borg-Warner, an automotive products firm, but closure of six bias-ply plants reduced its total capacity by 45 percent between 1978 and 1982.

General Tire closed only one plant, maintained overall capacity, and expanded market share. The most acute financial problems were encountered by Goodrich and U.S. Rubber (the latter had been renamed Uniroyal in 1966). Goodrich's OE market share drifted down after 1970, and the firm slipped into fourth place behind General Tire. Uniroyal's GM contracts ensured a healthy OE market share, but exposed the firm to the full effects of the depressed car industry and the costly switch to radials. Like General, Uniroyal's replacement sales were relatively poor. The firm experienced heavy losses in 1979 and 1980 and followed Firestone in slashing overall capacity drastically.

The advent of radials provided an opportunity for Michelin to return to the U.S. market. The firm became the first new OE supplier in 15 years when it obtained a Ford contract in 1970. Mastery of radial technology made the French firm a far more potent rival than its pre-1930 presence. Progress was slow, however. Michelin's OE share was below 2 percent in 1975, but construction of a factory at Greenville, South Carolina, in 1976 and a Chrysler contract a year later signaled a more determined effort. Michelin also became a force in the replacement sector; its market share expanded from 1.5 percent to 7 percent between 1972 and 1980. This new competition placed greater pressure on domestic firms. Product innovation encouraged only one other new entrant: International Rubber Industries (IRI) established a Kentucky factory in 1974 and aimed to offset low volume with high-quality, expensive steel-belted radials.

The advent of radials was a challenge that deterred or defeated some existing producers because of the cost of new investment and the increased significance of economies of scale. As early as 1973, Gates

Rubber concluded that its 3 percent market share did not justify the expense of developing steel-belted radials, and the firm abandoned passenger tires in favor of a general rubber goods trade. Thereafter, the acceptance of radials progressively squeezed smaller companies' bias tire sales. Denman ceased passenger tire output in 1975, and McCreary quit the passenger tire business in 1980.

Other small firms initiated radial production with varying degrees of success. Mansfield developed its own radials, but its contract to supply Firestone was wound down. Following heavy losses, Mansfield closed its Tupelo plant and quit tire manufacturing in 1979. IRI closed in 1980 after only six years; the industry's swift adoption of radials, and the general recession undermined its high price strategy. For Mohawk the loss of important private brand contracts precipitated a crisis in 1978. The firm closed its high-cost Akron plant and a year later shut an Arkansas factory following a labor dispute. Production was concentrated in Salem, Virginia, and Mohawk reduced its range of tires and dealerships. The firm maintained a 1 percent share of the replacement market while promoting sales of tread rubber and industrial goods.

Cooper and Armstrong were more successful. Cooper's share of the replacement market actually increased from 0.8 percent in 1972 to 2.5 percent a decade later. The company licensed foreign technology to achieve the transition to radial tires and supplemented the capacity of its Ohio and Arkansas factories by purchasing Mansfield's defunct Tupelo plant in 1984. Armstrong retained its vital cost-plus contract with Sears, which accounted for 40 percent of Armstrong's sales in 1981, and extended its other private brand business. During the 1970s the firm widened national dealer distribution of its own brand but still had no company stores. In 1974 Armstrong acquired Gates's brand name plus the new Nashville factory, but it closed its own West Haven plant in 1980 after a loss of $16.4 million. The firm's replacement market share increased from 1 percent in the early 1970s to between 2 percent and 2.5 percent in the 1980s. In part, surviving small firms gained from the withdrawal of other marginal firms, but longer-term success depended on developing radials and maintaining private brand business.

☐ Federal Tire Grading

Other influences added to the emphasis on the product. In the 1950s a small band of surgeons, local officials, and congressmen initiated a debate about automobile design, safety, and advertising. Tires were a minor element in this broader concern. From the 1920s automobiles had increased in power, weight, and size, and once demand stabilized after the postwar boom, further spectacular increases prompted claims that some fully loaded vehicles exceeded the carrying capacity of their tires. More powerful cars and faster speeds on the new federal highways certainly placed greater strain on tires. In the 1950s the National Tire Dealers and Retreaders Association (NTDRA) cited safety, along with the low profit margins, in a campaign against fourth-line tires. Both NTDRA and the Department of Commerce advocated standardization to counter the proliferation of tire sizes, designs, and prices. The Federal Trade Commission issued guidance on tire advertising and labeling in 1958. Senator Hubert Humphrey referred to the idea of grading and safety standards during hearings on tire distribution a year later, and in 1962 the FTC requested information on tire quality with a view to providing guidance to consumers. The industry's move from four to two plies of tire cord provoked questions about the relative strengths of different tires.

Manufacturers pointed to existing OE tire specifications published by the Tire and Rim Association. The Rubber Manufacturers' Association successfully opposed tire safety standards proposed by the state of New York. However, as several states debated tire safety, the RMA introduced voluntary standards in 1965 for tire strength, endurance, and high-speed performance. The plan, adapted from federal purchasing specifications, relied on self-certification by manufacturers, a central tire directory, and limited random testing by private laboratories. External discussion continued. In 1965 the FTC held hearings on tire advertising, sizes, and quality, and congressional hearings were held on a bill for tire grading and labeling according to uniform standards. Wisconsin Senator Gaylord Nelson emerged as the leading proponent of tire legislation.

RMA president Ross Ormsby, emphasizing improvements in tire life, suggested that neglect and poor driving posed more serious safety problems than tire defects. He highlighted the difficulties of establishing uniform standards given inevitable variations in driving conditions and tire wear. Ormsby suggested that the RMA's voluntary regulations were adequate, but he favored state rather than federal legislation. The NTDRA agreed that grading was impractical, but advocated standardization of sizes and descriptions, and the FTC urged minimum safety standards. RMA standards were criticized as minimal and lacking effective enforcement, and all sides agreed on the need for further research into tire performance.

The issue of tire safety was then overshadowed by the criticisms, notably in the Ribicoff hearings, of unsafe vehicle designs and accident rates. The car industry's uncertain response and General Motors's overreaction to Ralph Nader paved the way for the National Traffic and Motor Vehicle Safety Act in 1966. A National Highway Traffic Safety Administration (NHTSA), within the Department of Transportation, was required to set safety standards for automobile design, including tires. NHTSA proposed uniform systems of tire grading in 1966, and the RMA responded with revised voluntary standards. In 1968 NHTSA's Standard No. 109 established minimum requirements for tire dimensions and performance; Standard No. 110 covered rims and tire loads. Truck tire standards were published in 1973. The federal scheme was derived from Society of Automotive Engineers' specifications for traction, temperature resistance, and tread wear. Like the earlier RMA scheme, Standard No. 109 relied on self-certification and random testing by commercial laboratories. The industry criticized the tests as inaccurate, unrepresentative of road conditions, and unduly expensive. Advocates of regulation complained about the weak enforcement powers, limited testing facilities, and self-certification.

Progress was made on tire wear. The RMA's new Tire Safety Council publicized tire safety. States established minimum tread depths, and government and industry encouraged inspections and conscientious tire maintenance. Manufacturers added tread-wear bars, which were revealed as the tread wore. Such publicity combined improved safety with the possibility of more frequent replacement orders.

Despite minimum standards, it proved difficult to establish a uniform tire quality grading system (UTQGS) that would distinguish between different tires. There was a round of proposal, criticism, and redrafting of federal and industry plans. Tire grading plans were advanced in 1971, scrapped in 1973, reintroduced in 1976, and subjected to legal challenges by the industry. Eventually grading of bias and bias-belted tires commenced in 1979, and radials, by then the principal design, were graded from 1980. The protracted delays limited the impact of the UTQGS. Manufacturers could select gradings below a tire's probable performance in order to lessen the risk of penalties. NHTSA stressed grading as an aid to consumer choice rather than either a safety rating or warranty. Generally the industry remained hostile to tire grading because of its potential use in competitors' advertising. In 1965 only McCreary spoke in favor, and the firm subsequently became a critic. In 1981 Uniroyal angered their competitors by comparing UTQGS ratings on some of its tires favorably in advertising with those of other manufacturers.

In contrast to automobiles, the 1966 act did not permit NHTSA to order the recall of defective or unsafe tires. Nonetheless, federal pressure persuaded Mohawk and General Tire to make voluntary recalls in 1969. The 1966 Act was amended in 1969 to make manufacturers responsible for tire recalls. Further legislation brought more detailed recall provisions. Between 1973 and 1986 there were an annual average of 25 recalls, which, in most years, involved less than 0.1 percent of tire sales. In 1974, 1978, and 1980, however, there were substantial recalls of certain tires. The outstanding episodes were the recall of Firestone's "500" steel-belted radials in 1978 and 1980 and of two million Uniroyal tires in 1980. Such recalls involved highly damaging publicity.

In 1972 an NHTSA investigation of Firestone's "500" bias tire finally concluded it met Standard No. 109. However, NHTSA then focused on tread separation problems with Firestone's new "500" steel-belted radial. Between 1972 and 1978 Firestone had manufactured 23.6 million "500" steelbelted radials, its premier tire, and supplied similar tires to General Motors, Montgomery Ward, and Shell. A company survey identified the "500" as the industry's best-known brand name in 1974. The "500" steel-belted radials passed standard No. 109 in a routine fashion, but in 1977 Firestone voluntarily recalled 400,000 tires under federal pressure. In the following year the tire was the subject of congressional and NHTSA hearings. Criticism centered on accidents involving sudden blowouts and incidents where the tread had broken away from the casing. A congressional report claimed that adjustment rates (the replacement of defective or prematurely worn tires) far exceeded those on Firestone's other lines or of other manufacturers. The report also recommended revising Standard No. 109 and the recall provisions.

John Floberg, Firestone's chief counsel, pointed out in congressional hearings that the "500" tire met Standard No. 109 and argued that failures were associated primarily with excessive speed or underinflation, which weakened a tire's internal structure. The high adjustment rates, Floberg asserted, reflected the company's generous policy on replacements and unusually large claims following the adverse publicity, while the radials' durability allowed more time in which accidents could occur. He stressed the company's quality control procedures, although other evidence suggested that Firestone experienced problems in the production of the "500" as well as quality control, and frequent adjustments with the "500" radials between 1972 and 1975, well before the public criticism. The firm settled out of court with the FTC following complaints that its advertising had not emphasized the importance of the careful maintenance on which Firestone had based its case. Central to Firestone's defense was the argument that any recall order required precise scientific evidence of a specific design defect or flaw rather than circumstantial evidence linking the tire to accidents and high adjustment rates.

Public hearings, media reports, and several product liability suits badly damaged Firestone's public image, and although never conceding that the "500" tire was defective, Firestone agreed to terms with the NHTSA for a voluntary recall in October 1978. Eight million tires produced since 1975 were to be replaced free of charge, while a further six million tires manufactured earlier were eligible for a half-price replacement. Production of the new "721" steel radial was expanded to provide replacements; the recall campaign cost an estimated $160 million. It was a costly and damaging episode, which weakened Firestone's public image, its finances, and self-confidence at a critical time in the adoption of radials. It appeared to confirm the suspicion that American manufacturers were inferior to overseas firms in radial technology. Equally, the case raised doubts about federal tire regulations. The "500" had satisfied Standard No. 109, and Firestone's defense revealed the NHTSA's uncertainty over its powers and the precise conditions for a recall. A recall involving two million Uniroyal tires in 1980 and another 164,000 in 1986 aggravated a second company's existing financial difficulties.

Since 1976 NHTSA has revived the earlier emphasis on driver education. In 1984 only a legal challenge prevented NHTSA from dropping its tread-wear standard, and tire registration has become voluntary for purchases from dealers, resulting in fewer registrations. Manufacturers have complained that tire standards impose excessive costs and are unnecessary given the small contribution of tire failure to accidents. Certainly the switch to radials dramatically improved tire wear, and new technology outstripped the minimum federal standards. Yet federal measures did promote a more systematic approach to product quality and encouraged advertisers to reemphasize safety, although it is doubtful whether tire gradings significantly altered the imperatives of price and brand loyalty.

☐ Competition and Multinational Acquisitions in the 1980s

From the low point of 146 million in 1980, unit sales revived slowly to 202 million tires in 1984, thereby regaining 1973 levels. The upturn was uneven. OE demand remained slack; car production declined to 1982 with automobile companies badly affected by a combination of declining sales and high interest rates. The "Big Three" car firms responded with layoffs and closures, and only federal support averted Chrysler's collapse. Traditionally strong OE customer relations persisted: Goodyear was the main supplier to Chrysler and American Motors, Firestone to Ford, and Uniroyal to General Motors. Goodrich, despite its early advocacy of radials, continued losing ground in the early 1970s and finally quit the OE market in 1982 (see Table 9.3). General Tire's OE market share expanded steadily, while Goodyear's share leapt 5 percent in 1975 when the firm finally acknowledged the need to concentrate on radials. At the same time, weak demand and Michelin's entry ensured low margins.

The 1979 oil crisis dramatically shifted consumer preference toward smaller, more fuel-efficient vehicles, and the domestic firms' inability to accommodate demand allowed Japanese imports to fill the gap. This weakening of their principal customers aggravated the impact of the domestic recessions in 1974–75, 1980, and 1982 for tire manufacturers. Imported cars were not a new phenomenon; their share of the U.S. market was 10 percent in 1959 and 15 percent in 1970, but reached 27 percent in 1980. Since imported vehicles were equipped with tires, they represented lost orders for U.S. producers unless their foreign subsidiaries captured the business. Japanese imports were a particular threat since U.S. companies made no OE sales there, and indigenous firms,

Table 9.3. Original Equipment Sales by Firm, 1965–87 (%)

Firm	1965	1970	1975	1980	1985	1987
Goodyear	30	32	35	28	32	33
Firestone	25	27	24	22	22	22
Uniroyal	24	18	20	24	—	—
B.F. Goodrich	17	16	8	10	—	—
Uniroyal-Goodrich	—	—	—	—	22	19
General Tire	4	7	12	11	13	13
Michelin	—	*	1	5	11	13
Pirelli	—	—	—	—	*	*
Continental	—	—	—	—	*	*
Dunlop	—	—	—	—	—	*

* < 1 percent Note: Percentages rounded to nearest whole number.

Sources: J. S. Dick "How Technological Innovations Have Affected the Tire Industry's Structure," *Elastomerics*, November 1980, 43, table 13. *Modern Tire Dealer*, "Annual Facts Directory," January 1973, 76; January 1976, 64; January 1981, 35; January 1985, 42; January 1988, 42.

notably Bridgestone, followed their vehicle manufacturers overseas with tire exports. The high value of the dollar, European recessions, and the earlier impact of radials overseas also encouraged European interest in the vast U.S. tire market. Imported tires accounted for 16 percent of the passenger tire market by 1984 compared to only 1 percent in 1967.

☐ Competition in the Replacement Market

Changing tire designs complicated pricing policy and, thus, profitability. An ascending price structure developed from bias to bias-belted and then up to radial tires. There were further variations according to size, materials, and marketing strategy; steel-belted radials, for example, were more expensive than other radials. Finally radials penetrated down from the higher-price performance tire markets into more general use. Bias tires retained an advantage for some drivers, especially of older cars for which radial durability was less important.

Further changes in tire size were required to accommodate the move to smaller cars in the late 1970s. At the same time higher prices were sought by promoting different tires on the basis of particular qualities, such as safety or style. In 1976 Goodyear introduced "all-season" tires; the tread was devised to cope with winter conditions and, thus, obviate the changeover to snow tires in northern states. As the industry adopted the idea, all-season tires increased from 2 percent of 1978 replacement sales to 55 percent by 1987. Their success further complicated pricing, and challenged all firms to maintain product development. New low-profile tires, or "performance" tires, were marketed as a means of improving handling on fast cars. The association with glamorous and expensive vehicles aided sales, and here the industry emphasized performance grades for marketing purposes, despite its general resistance to tire grading.

In general, excess capacity promoted price competition. In 1975 Goodrich priced its first-line tires below those of other leading manufacturers, which narrowed differentials generally, and subsidiaries, such as Goodyear's Lee and Firestone's Dayton, contributed to competition for second-line and private-brand orders. The settlement of the lengthy strike in 1976 was followed by competition to regain market share. Narrowing price differentials and increased competition in the lower-price sector were perpetuated by excess capacity during 1978. Margins and price differentials between major and private brands probably narrowed in the 1970s, although variations in product mix and the accounting treatment of raw material costs hinder a precise judgment. The advent of radials encouraged a new bout of warranty competition.

Replacement sales rebounded from the 1980 recession, but despite the wave of plant closures, unused capacity remained and prices fell after 1981. The cost of one radial tire averaged $51.80 by 1987 compared with $72.71 in 1980, and the premium between radial and other tires declined. In 1984 *Rubber Trends* reported that "price cutting and discounting are rife" and profits declined as firms struggled for volume.

Surprisingly, after 40 years of decline, the independent dealers' share of replacement sales rose from 39 percent in 1964 to 55 percent in 1971, and to 65 percent a decade later (see Table 9.4). Dealers benefited from their role in distributing the rising volume of imported tires and a tendency toward multiple dealerships. Some dealers formed buying groups to obtain better terms. The dealers' resurgence was at the expense of oil company service stations and, less markedly, chain and department stores: oil companies held only 5 percent of replacement sales in 1980 compared to around 25 percent in the early 1950s. As tire demand slackened and their other lines yielded higher profits, oil companies shifted from full auto service to self-service gas stations.

Manufacturers paid greater attention to replacement business as OE sales slackened. Goodyear (in 1968) and Firestone (in 1971) introduced franchised Tire Centers and, along with General and Uniroyal, added more company stores. The company stores' share of replacement sales remained close to their position in the 1930s, but by the 1980s strategies varied. Firestone and Goodyear retained large retail chains, and Michelin finally supported its American expansion through the acquisition of company stores. Firestone emphasized full auto servicing

Table 9.4. Distribution of Replacement Tire Sales, 1964–87 (%)

Year	Independent Dealers	Mail-Order Chain Stores	Company Stores	Department Stores	Oil Companies
1964	38.8	22.4	10.3	5.0	23.5
1971	55.0	16.5	9.4	3.6	15.5
1975	55.5	16.5	11.0	2.5	14.5
1981	65.0	20.0	10.0	*	5.0
1987	68.0	17.0	13.0	*	2.0

* included in mail-order and chain stores from 1977

Sources: 1964 figures: Federal Trade Commission, *Economic Report on the Manufacture and Distribution of Automotive Tires*, 109, appendix table 14; 1971–87 figures: *Modern Tire Dealer*, "Annual Facts Directory," January 1972, 55; January 1981, 39; January 1986, 58; January 1988, 46.

through its stores, Tire Centers, and dealers as a strategy for maximizing returns from the replacement sector at a time when motorists were less inclined to buy new cars.

Other leading firms retreated from retailing in favor of reliance on dealers. In 1985 Goodrich sold 110 of its 165 retail stores, and Uniroyal and General Tire also closed stores, having failed to convert OE sales into comparable replacement business. Goodrich concentrated on the replacement market, particularly high-performance tires, and regarded company stores as too expensive for this niche marketing strategy. Among leading retailers, strategies were mixed: K-mart closed some smaller auto service stations, while Sears expanded by acquiring Western Auto Supply. A new feature were warehouse clubs specializing in low prices and minimum service.

□   Specialist Tires and Diversification

Passenger tires accounted for 56 percent of industry sales in 1977, but only 46 of 200 tire plants. The other major sector was truck and bus tires, some 28 percent of industry sales, while miscellaneous tires provided another 8 percent. Most manufacturers supplied several types of tires in order to apply their expertise widely. Generally, the leading firms produced the full range of tires, although Goodrich and Uniroyal retreated from several markets in the 1980s. Small firms increasingly sought niches in specialist sectors where economies of scale were less important.

Each tire market possessed its own characteristics. Over 90 percent of aircraft tire sales were replacements. Retreading was a major element in the market because aircraft treads wore rapidly compared with their casings. Retreads accounted for around one-third of replacement sales of large truck tires in the early 1980s. Conversely, the RV (recreational vehicle) tire business was almost entirely based on sales to vehicle manufacturers. Competition in the industrial tire market took the form of an extensive product range designed for specific vehicles and equipment.

All tire markets were affected by general economic trends, but also responded to discrete influences. The farm tire business experienced the "boom-and-bust" cycle characteristic of the farm economy in the 1970s and 1980s. A sellers' market in the early 1970s provided a lucrative alternative to the depressed passenger tire sector. Within a decade, however, falling farm prices and increased indebtedness had reduced purchases of farm machinery. Tire sales were particularly poor in 1983. The industrial tire market was also volatile with demand dependent on the business cycle and, thus, depressed in the mid-1970s and early 1980s, but stronger from 1983 to 1988. Aircraft tire demand—divided between commercial, freight, and military customers—was subject to many influences. Sales fluctuated, with a postwar record of 1 million units in 1968, but slumped as the U.S. withdrew from Vietnam and recessions affected civilian orders.

During the 1970s many firms expanded their interest in truck and bus tires, which had lower unit sales, but higher added value and profits. Truck and bus markets displayed similar patterns of powerful OE buyers, a complex leasing and fleet market, and replacement sales, including Sears and other private brands. There were two distinct sectors: light versus medium and heavy truck tires and, compared with passenger tires, a sizable retreading and servicing sector.

Although precise shares varied, the five major producers dominated most sectors, notably OE sales and the leasing of tires to bus lines. In 1981 Goodyear held 14 percent and its Kelly-Springfield subsidiary 10 percent of light truck tire sales, and the two combined supplied 28 percent of larger truck tire sales. Firestone was also prominent. Nonetheless, middling and small firms obtained significant shares of sales. Cooper, Armstrong, Dunlop, and General each held between 5 percent and 7 percent of the medium truck tire market in the 1980s. From 1975 Denman concentrated on short production runs of light truck tires, and Mohawk increased its sales, acting as a distributor for Michelin. The recessions of the 1980s brought some changes. McCreary abandoned medium-tire production due to price competition, and Armstrong's Natchez truck tire plant was sold to a group of employees in 1986. Goodrich's closure of the Miami, Oklahoma, plant signaled withdrawal from heavy-duty truck tire production, and Uniroyal followed suit.

Overseas producers often entered the U.S. market in the truck tire trade. Michelin became a leading producer, while Bridgestone and other Japanese companies obtained smaller market shares. The entry of foreign companies reflected a move toward radial truck tires, which slowed the growth of replacement demand by the 1980s. Foreign competition was a factor in other tire markets. As Japanese firms took the lead in the motorcycle industry so tire imports increased. Goodyear abandoned motorcycle tires in 1982, leaving Carlisle, Dunlop, and Denman as the only U.S.-based producers, with Bridgestone, Continental, and Michelin the main importers. A similar pattern developed in the bicycle tire trade: Carlisle, the leading U.S. firm, announced its withdrawal in 1987 in the face of Asian imports.

After 1970 some small firms, such as McCreary, retreated from the passenger tire market into specialist tire production. Such products offered higher profits and production-to-order, which a small firm could provide. Companies such as Denman, Cooper, and McCreary increasingly emphasized such specialist production for mining, farm, vintage, and four-wheel-drive vehicles. McCreary began manufacturing aircraft, industrial, farm, garden equipment, and trailer tires. Other small companies, for example, specialized manufacturers and distributors of industrial tires, such as Bearcat Tire and Teledyne Monarch, developed a particular market niche. Many small producers concentrated on semipneumatic and solid tires for industrial equipment, often using plastics or nonrubber compounds. Such business sustained a large number of small establishments within a highly concentrated industry. Related sectors were "off-the-road" tires for buggies, trailers, other vehicles, and mobile homes. Yet more specialized was the manufacture of reproduction tires for antique or classic cars. Denman, McCreary, and specialist companies, such as the Universal Tire Company, produced tires copying earlier sizes and wheel, rim, tread, and sidewall designs. In some cases larger firms decided that the smaller tire markets were unattractive: Goodrich and Uniroyal abandoned off-the-road and farm tires after the 1982 recession.

A further strategy was to avoid direct competition with the major manufacturers even within specialist markets. By the 1980s there were four manufacturers of aircraft tires: Goodyear, Goodrich, Thompson Aircraft Tires, and McCreary. The last concentrated on light aircraft tires, while Thompson emphasized retreading and marketed Bridgestone tires. Production of racing tires was dominated by Goodyear, Firestone, and McCreary. The last concentrated on smaller race tracks, while the majors supplied a full range of racing tires. There were also specialists such as Hoosier Racing Tire Co., which began as a distributor of Mohawk go-cart and stock car tires. Hoosier opened its own plant when Mohawk closed its Akron factory in 1978. Larger truck and farm tires and many off-the-road tires still used inner tubes, and in 1983 there were 28 firms that manufactured and distributed inner tubes. No firm supplied a complete range. Firestone, Goodyear, Armstrong, and Carlisle had the widest range, while some companies concentrated on specific markets: Bearcat Tire (industrial) or Lee (agricultural and truck). There were some inner tube producers who did not also make tires, notably Polson Rubber and Indianapolis Rubber.

A further option was to develop nontire business either within the rubber industry or in unrelated areas. There was a rough division according to the degree of specialization. The small or medium-size firms, such as Armstrong and Cooper, relied most heavily on tires that constituted between 70 percent and 100 percent of their sales. The leading producers, Goodyear and Firestone, had around 70 percent of their business in tires, while their closest rivals, Goodrich, Uniroyal, and General Tire, were more diversified with between 30 percent and 50 percent of their sales provided by tires. The majority of firms possessed mechanical goods divisions, although these often relied heavily on sales of automotive parts or industrial goods and, therefore, provided little respite from the impact of recessions. Cooper manufactured mechanical and molded rubber goods and industrial machinery; the firm also operated a technical services division to apply its expertise in rubber technology in response to any form of customer request. From the 1940s there had been rapid development of rubber or polymer-related technologies such as roofing, waterproofing materials, and plastics. Such alternative markets could become highly competitive owing to frequent innovation and the relative ease of entry for small rubber firms, as well as existing chemicals or plastics companies.

The poor returns in many tire markets encouraged diversification to promote earnings. The traditionally more diversified of the major companies placed greatest emphasis on this strategy. After the 1982 recession General Tire emphasized its nontire activities and two years later reorganized as GenCorp with four divisions: Aerojet General, RKO General, DiversiTech General, and General Tire. DiversiTech General covered chemicals and plastics, while RKO General included soft drink bottling. Goodrich bolstered its chemicals and plastics divisions. Goodyear also diversified by purchasing Celeron, an oil and natural gas producer, and became involved in the completion of an oil pipeline from the Gulf coast to California. Conversely, Firestone's desire to reduce debt led to the sale of its defense products group in 1982 and its plastics division in 1981. The firm was, thus, even more dependent on the automotive sector.

☐ Reorganization

Given a poor performance since 1973, passenger tire production was beset with doubts. With dividends low, manufacturers were vulnerable. In 1969 Goodrich fought off a takeover bid by Northwestern Industries, and Firestone decided against a merger with Borg-Warner in the aftermath of the "500" recall a decade later. The stock market boom of the 1980s brought new threats. Goodrich and Uniroyal resisted speculative stock purchases by Carl Icahn in 1984 and 1985, and GenCorp survived a hostile bid in 1987. Even Goodyear was not immune; ironically its diversification proved a liability. Financier Sir James Goldsmith acquired a stake in the firm, criticized Goodyear's investments in the oil and gas industries, and proclaimed the need to concentrate on the core tire business. Certainly the costs of an oil pipeline investment contributed to the low dividends that made Goodyear vulnerable. In November 1987 Goodyear averted Goldsmith's bid by purchasing his stock.

The initial impact of the speculative bids was retrenchment as managements tried to improve immediate earnings and service debts. Following Goldsmith's withdrawal, Goodyear had $4 billion of indebtedness and was forced to dispose of Goodyear Aerospace, Motor Wheel, and the Celeron pipeline interests, as well as real estate in Arizona. After resisting Icahn, Uniroyal's management organized a buyout through Clayton and Dubilier, a New York firm specializing in leveraged buyouts, and sold many subsidiaries including chemicals and transmission belting divisions. Such defensive moves did not remove underlying problems of unused tire capacity and often left the firms less diversified.

A more extensive restructuring followed through a series of mergers and acquisitions that produced the industry's most profound reorganization since the interwar years. In 1986 Uniroyal and Goodrich combined their tire operations, excluding aircraft tires, in the jointly owned Uniroyal Goodrich Tire Company (UGTC). The logic was to match Uniroyal's strength in the OE sector with Goodrich's larger replacement business, while leaving the two parent companies to develop their other more profitable divisions. However, UGTC had a large debt burden and lost $46 million in its first full year of operations. The firm's OE market share declined, and a clash of management styles was reported between the two halves of the business. In December 1987 Goodrich sold its holding to Clayton and Dubilier.

Smaller firms were also reorganized. In 1987 the group of Armstrong companies was renamed the Armtek Corporation, Mohawk was acquired by the Danaher Corp. in 1984 and resold four years later, and Denman was purchased by the Jepson Corp. in 1987. In 1986 McCreary's Indiana plant lost $2.8 million, and a lengthy dispute led to URW labor being replaced by nonunion labor. A year later, after financial problems, Polymer Enterprises was created as a holding company for McCreary's separate tire and industrial products divisions.

The mid-1980s saw even greater changes. When its parent company was dismembered following a financial crisis, Dunlop Tire of America was purchased by a consortium, including its existing management, and operated as an independent unit. Then, in 1987, GenCorp sold its General Tire division to Continental, the major German tire firm. A year later Bridgestone, the leading Japanese producer, acquired Firestone. Pirelli, which had bid for both General Tire and Firestone, then purchased Armtek's tire division. In 1989 Michelin declared its intention to purchase UGTC in 1990. The plan offered Michelin a stronger position in the OE and private brand sectors. It had the potential to trigger renewed price competition by giving the French firm a greater stake in the low-priced tire market without undermining its own brand's reputation for quality and high prices. These changes completed the earlier strategies of diversification. GenCorp concentrated on its aviation, entertainment, plastics, and bottling subsidiaries, and Goodrich's business was now based on plastics, chemicals, and defense products. Goodyear, the only remaining major domestic tire firm, now faced powerful local competition from multinational rivals.

10

Multinational Enterprise in the Tire Industry

THE PRESENT TIRE BUSINESS IS OFTEN DE-
scribed as a "global" industry in which a few multinational enterprises
increasingly dominate the world market and seek to use similar products
and marketing strategies in all areas. The competitive pressures found
in domestic markets now operate on a broader stage. This situation is
the outcome of a complex and fluctuating process that began in the
nineteenth century. Rubber manufacturing always possessed an international character because the industry relied on imported natural rubber
until the advent of all-purpose synthetic rubbers. Even after 1940 natural rubber remained significant, and the oil required for synthetics was
also traded on world commodity markets. Manufacturers operated overseas through a mix of exporting, patent licensing, technical assistance to
other producers, and direct investments in factories.

Such activities were present in the nineteenth century, but received
added impetus from the advent of tires, the international spread of car
ownership, and foreign investments by automobile manufacturers.
American companies encountered major overseas rivals, notable Michelin (France), Dunlop (Britain), Pirelli (Italy), and, in recent years,
Bridgestone (Japan). These firms were, in turn, active to varying degrees in the U.S. market. By 1990 Goodyear, Michelin, and Bridgestone
were established as the dominant producers for the U.S. market, and
several major U.S. firms had passed into foreign ownership.

☐ Natural Rubber Supply and Multinational Investment

In the nineteenth century natural rubber, the basic raw material, was obtained primarily through imports from South America and, on a smaller scale, from Africa. Rubber was sold through local middlemen and then shipped to London, European ports, or New York, where manufacturers purchased supplies through rubber brokers or dealers who graded the rubber by its origin and quality. Output expanded rapidly, but there were limits to the efficiency of the wild rubber system of collecting rubber from scattered trees, especially since tapping was forced further inland with consequent increases in transport costs.

In 1876 Henry Wickham shipped a consignment of Hevea seeds from South America to London, and seedlings were later transferred to British colonial possessions in Ceylon and Singapore. These steps had no immediate commercial impact, although modest interest in rubber planting was stimulated by low prices of tea and coffee, the existing plantation crops, during the 1890s. After 1900 increasing demand for tires and other rubber goods led to rising rubber prices and a burst of planting in Southeast Asia. The newly planted trees took several years to mature and begin yielding rubber, so sustained growth of demand and the inefficiencies of wild rubber collection drove prices to record levels by 1910, producing a European mania for plantation investments. The sheer scale of planting and the greater ease of cultivation, tapping, and distribution of plantation rubber became evident in a dramatic fashion.

The great southeast Asian plantation regions were barely in production in 1910, but within five years these new producers accounted for two-thirds of total output and the wild rubber industry was in decline. An additional influence was the spread of rubber cultivation on locally owned smallholdings, a highly efficient, low-cost source, which undermined plantation companies' hopes of substantial profits. Rubber prices remained volatile, but average prices in New York fell from $2.06 per pound in 1910 to 65 cents per pound in 1914. Manufacturers benefited from declining costs once they had adjusted to using plantation rubber.

The British Dunlop company built up the most extensive plantation investments by 1914. U.S. manufacturers generally ignored early American ventures into rubber growing, which included the establishment of a guayule plantation in Mexico. U.S. Rubber had decided against purchasing a wild rubber concession in Brazil in 1903, but escalating prices persuaded the firm to lease 83,000 acres of partially cleared land in Sumatra in 1909. U.S. Rubber was influenced by Edgar Davis, an assiduous promoter of the idea of American plantation investment, but other manufacturers delayed investment as rubber prices declined.

World War I dislocated the Eurocentric shipping, trade, and financial system for rubber, and a British embargo on rubber exports threatened supplies in December 1914. U.S. manufacturers and dealers dispatched representatives to London, and the embargo was lifted in return for commitments not to supply Germany. Rubber imports were maintained during the war through greater use of Japanese shipping and a temporary revival in wild rubber output; consumption of recycled rubber also increased substantially. Nonetheless, the war emphasized America's dependence, as the consumer of 60 percent of world production, on overseas sources under British and European influence. The principal response of the major U.S. firms was to bypass the London markets by establishing purchasing organizations in Singapore. Firestone and Goodrich limited themselves to such overseas purchasing. However, U.S. Rubber extended its plantations and was joined by Goodyear, which purchased 20,000 acres in Dutch-ruled Sumatra in 1916. Goodyear's earlier confidence that market forces would lower prices had given way to concern about potential supply restrictions. Davis, thwarted in his desire for even greater investment by U.S. Rubber, created a new venture, the International Plantation Rubber Company, and urged the merger of U.S. Rubber and Goodyear's holdings. The scheme did not materialize, however. Wartime investments were motivated by a desire for continuity of supply in the long-term and had little immediate impact. Only half of U.S. Rubber's site, acquired in 1910, was in production in 1922, and Goodyear's plantation did not yield rubber until 1923.

The 1920–21 recession highlighted the manufacturers' financial vulnerability to simultaneous falls in rubber prices and tire demand. It also underlined the vast natural rubber capacity created during the previous 15 years of speculative planting. In 1921 rubber prices were only 10 percent of their 1910 level, and planter dissatisfaction led the British to introduce export restrictions in Malaya and Ceylon in an effort to raise prices. The Stevenson Act operated from 1922 to 1928 and initially limited exports to 60 percent of 1920 production. Harvey Firestone attacked the scheme bitterly and became a zealous convert to Davis's ideal of American plantation ownership. Other manufacturers and the Rubber Manufacturers' Association were prepared to accept higher prices and costs if the Stevenson Act brought stable prices. All parties were to be disappointed. Prices were held above their market level, but British planters lost market share to producers in the Dutch colonial possessions where output from locally owned plantations and smallholdings also expanded. The British restriction plan was finally abandoned in 1928.

Prices did not stabilize. In 1925 demand rose immediately after a reduction in export quotas and rubber prices nearly tripled. In response a rubber-buying pool was formed in 1926 involving U.S. Rubber, Goodyear, Goodrich, Firestone, Fisk, and General Motors. The intention was to use the firms' combined purchasing power to moderate price fluctuations, but the pool was abandoned in 1928 as declining rubber prices reduced the value of its reserves.

American manufacturers expanded direct investment with active encouragement from the U.S. Department of Commerce, which inveighed against foreign "monopolies" in essential materials. Firestone had leased a small Liberian plantation in 1925 following extended bargaining with the Monrovian government. U.S. Rubber had 54,053 acres in production by 1927, and Goodyear acquired a plantation in the Philippines, a country outside British influence and, thus, not affected by the restriction scheme, in 1928. The most curious episode was the Ford Motor Company's decision to establish plantations in Brazil in 1927. It proved an expensive failure because the rows of young trees were irresistible to indigenous pests, and the terrain, labor, transport, and management posed further problems. Despite a net loss of $7.8 million, Ford's plantations continued until 1945.

Rubber prices slipped from 72.5 cents per pound in 1926 to 20.5 cents in 1929 and then slumped to only 3.5 cents three years later as economic activity collapsed in the face of the international depression. These debilitating conditions induced new supply restrictions in the form of the International Rubber Regulation Agreement (IRRA) in 1934. The plan, covering 98 percent of world production, was far more comprehensive than the Stevenson Act and limited shipments from American-owned plantations in southeast Asia. To get around this restriction, Goodyear acquired experimental sites in Panama and Costa Rica. IRRA again held prices above market levels without achieving the desired stability.

Japan's invasion of southeast Asia in 1942 ensured the loss of U.S. Rubber and Goodyear's investments. Firestone increased output from Liberia, and there was a flurry of interest in the dubious merits of cultivating rubber-bearing shrubs in the United States. The crucial development was the government's creation of the synthetic rubber industry, which eventually provided an all-purpose substitute for natural rubber. Tire producers' movement into synthetic rubber production was more common than plantation investment, especially as the government encouraged consortia of smaller producers to operate synthetic rubber plants. The result was a domestic source of the industry's main raw material and some respite from the volatile market for natural rubber. Yet plantation investments continued. U.S. Rubber, Goodyear, and Firestone extended their holdings, and Goodrich acquired its first plantation in 1954 and later obtained one in the Philippines. By the 1970s Firestone's original Liberian operations had been supplemented by plantations in Ghana, the Philippines, and Brazil, although the last was sold in 1984. Goodyear had plantations in the Philippines, Indonesia, Guatemala, and Brazil. U.S. Rubber's Malaysian investments were sold to a government agency in 1985 under a law requiring majority Malaysian ownership of rubber plantations.

Plantation investments were defensive responses to high prices around 1910 and supply constraints during World War I and in the 1920s and 1930s. U.S. Rubber amassed the largest American-owned holdings in this period and supplied 20 percent of its own rubber by 1925. U.S. Rubber Plantations Inc. was more profitable than its parent company in the 1920s, and DuPont's acquisition of U.S. Rubber was initially motivated by their assessment of the value of its plantation investments. The DuPonts even contemplated selling or leasing the tire plants in order to concentrate on rubber growing. There was a renewed proposal from the ubiquitous Edgar Davis for combining Goodyear's and U.S. Rubber's holdings as the basis of a large American plantation venture. Again the scheme failed to materialize.

Despite such indications of good returns, U.S. Rubber's inventory losses, outside of its plantations, exceeded those of any other manufacturer in the 1920s, and thereafter IRRA limited exports from the firm's plantations during the 1930s. Goodyear made several attempts to enter new plantation frontiers outside the control programs, yet the firm obtained only 10 percent of its total requirements from its own plantations in 1934. Firestone's Liberian venture was suspended between 1929 and 1934 when rubber prices plummeted. The manufacturers' overseas purchasing and forward contracts for rubber had a far more significant influence than plantations on rubber costs; recycled rubber and cost-plus contracts provided further counters to fluctuating rubber prices.

Plantation ownership did have the value of permitting experimental work on specialist rubbers, and since the availability of synthetic rubber did not completely remove the need for natural rubber, advances in rubber growing enhanced firms' ability to supply natural rubber for specific functions. Indeed, as the proportion of natural rubber in total consumption diminished, major firms could meet a greater percentage of their needs from their own resources.

However, since 1973 the consumption of natural rubber has increased because it performs better than synthetics in the radial tire's sidewalls. At the same time the earlier escape from restrictions on rubber supply was offset by OPEC, which raised oil, and thus synthetic rubber, prices. Natural rubber experienced a revival. Even so, manufacturers still purchased the bulk of their natural rubber on world markets, and their own plantations filled only a small portion of consumption. The traditional volatility of rubber prices continued in the face of the recessions of the 1970s and interest in supply restriction resurfaced. In 1976 rubber producers discussed the creation of a buffer stock to be used to raise prices and moderate price movements. In 1980 the International Natural Rubber Agreement began operations with the aim of maintaining a target price range, but the weak commodity markets of the early 1980s prevented the realization of that goal.

☐ Production Overseas

In contrast to the available limited analyses of plantation investments, Peter West's study assesses fully the tire industry's multinational manufacturing activities, and this account draws heavily on his work. In raw material supply, overseas activities concentrated on buying and growing rubber. On the production side, patent licensing, technical agreements, exports, overseas sales organizations, and direct investment in factories all contributed to the industry's international character. There was a flow of knowledge about rubber technology and products from the 1830s. In the early stages patent rights often inhibited international competition, just as they restricted the entry of domestic producers. For example, Charles Goodyear was unable to establish his vulcanization patent in England against the rival claims of Thomas Hancock. Yet there were suggestions that Hancock had succeeded by analyzing an early sample of Goodyear's vulcanized rubber. Following the development of bicycle tire production, dozens of patents for solid and pneumatic tire designs jostled for legal precedence and royalty income from licensing foreign manufacturers in the 1890s. The Bartlett and Gormully and Jeffrey tire patents established primacy over the clincher principle in Britain and the United States, respectively, after lengthy litigation. There was some interchange of technology, as when Goodrich purchased Palmer's cord tire patents in 1898. Equally, patent rights could lead to a divergence in technology. U.S. cycle tires followed the single-tube principle, while European producers generally adopted a double-tube cycle tire.

European rubber manufacturers developed extensive export sales in the nineteenth century, and in the case of footwear they even met to discuss pricing policies. The European firms also sold mechanical and other rubber goods widely overseas, and later they sold tires. American exports of rubber goods and later tires were small however. Overseas direct investment was also limited. American interests established the Hutchinson (Paris) and North British Rubber (Edinburgh) companies in the 1850s, but both of these rubber footwear ventures later passed into local ownership.

The bicycle craze of the 1890s produced a flurry of exporting by European tire manufacturers and the first major multinational investments. U.S. producers entered this process late because of their distance from the main European markets, Dunlop's control of major British patents, and American inferiority in pneumatic tire technology. Dunlop was the most active multinational establishing joint ventures in France and Germany in 1892; local manufacture was essential to establish patent claims. The French and German ventures became full subsidiaries in 1909 and 1910. In the United States, Dunlop first licensed a local producer and then in 1893 established the American Dunlop Company with a plant in New York. However, the American firm was sold five years later to finance Dunlop's domestic expansion and became part of the Rubber Goods Manufacturing Company. In 1909 Dunlop began a joint venture in Japan. While Dunlop sought to exploit its cycle tire patents and expertise, Michelin relied on exports until the growth of car tire demand, an area where the French firm was superior to Dunlop and, before 1906, to U.S. manufacturers. Michelin opened factories in Italy and the United States in 1907.

The first American tire manufacturer to move abroad was U.S. Rubber, which had a Canadian factory in 1907. Three years later Goodyear and Goodrich began production in Canada and France, respectively. American firms began to extend their sales organizations, particularly in Canada and Western Europe. The rapid growth of tire demand provided an incentive to foreign investments, and major advances in U.S. tire design between 1906 and 1909 strengthened American producers and dulled the impact of Michelin's New York factory.

World War I was an important stage in the tire industry's multinational development because the conflict restricted the exports of Dunlop, Michelin, Pirelli, and Continental (Germany). The interruption enabled U.S. manufacturers to exploit their ability to maintain supplies. The leading American companies further extended their overseas sales branches, and although still small relative to domestic sales, the American share of world tire exports increased from 7 percent to 36 percent between 1912 and 1919. Thereafter multinational rivalry became more pronounced and a defense of the newly captured export markets more likely. West identified 13 multinational investments in tire factories, all in developed economies between 1914 and 1929, of which 8 were by U.S. firms. Firestone (1919) and Goodrich (1923) opened Canadian plants, while Goodrich established shareholdings and technical agreements with Yokohama Rubber (Japan) and Continental. Goodyear built an Australian factory in 1927.

The focus of multinational investment in the 1920s, however, was Britain. Several firms possessed marketing subsidiaries in Britain before 1914 and the volume of postwar imports led Dunlop and other local producers to seek protection. In 1927 a 33 percent duty was placed on tire imports. Goodrich had a British plant after 1924, and the imposition of the tariff triggered the construction of factories by Michelin, Pirelli, Goodyear, and Firestone during 1927 and 1928. Protectionism determined the timing of these investments to protect sales in Britain and access to imperial markets. Equally, the swiftness and scale of entry emphasized the oligopolistic rivalry between the major national producers. Dunlop's decision to return to the U.S. market by opening a factory at Buffalo in 1923 reflected this element. Further stimuli were the multinational expansion of Ford and General Motors and their preference for local suppliers in response to emergent economic nationalism. Goodyear and Firestone, as the largest OE manufacturers, had every incentive to follow their customers overseas.

The depression of the 1930s created a mixed pattern. Some multinational firms retreated. Michelin closed its New York factory, and Goodrich sold its British subsidiary and its German and Japanese investments. U.S. Rubber closed several overseas branches and saw its export business decline in the face of weak demand and widespread protectionism. U.S. Rubber, Goodrich, General Tire, and Seiberling did participate in technical agreements in which they supplied tire designs and/or manufacturing expertise to smaller overseas producers. At the same time, West identified 21 new overseas ventures between 1930 and 1939. Goodyear added factories in Java, Brazil, and Sweden; Firestone entered Brazil, Spain, Switzerland, South Africa, and India; Dunlop opened plants in South Africa, India, and Eire; and Michelin consolidated its European base with investments in Germany, Belgium, and Spain.

The overall expansion of multinational investment was primarily a response to protectionism. Firms used local factories to substitute for imports, but oligopolistic rivalry was also important, particularly in Argentina where Firestone, Michelin, and Goodyear all built factories to prevent one firm from dominating the market. The spate of plant construction created excess capacity and strained resources given the financial stringency of the 1930s. There were attempts to agree on export prices in the late 1920s, but the principal solution was for one firm's overseas factory to supply another's local marketing organization. In 1934 Dunlop agreed to supply Goodyear dealers from its South African, Indian, and Irish factories; in return Goodyear produced Dunlop tires in Argentina, Brazil, Java, and Sweden. Each firm provided tire molds for the partner's factory. West discovered the arrangement still in operation in Argentina and Peru in the mid-1970s. In 1939 Firestone agreed to supply tires for U.S. Rubber in Argentina, while Pirelli and U.S. Rubber operated a joint venture in that country between 1951 and 1968. U.S. Rubber's export division contracted for tires with Gislaved in Sweden and North British Rubber in Britain in the 1930s. Such arrangements fell midway between technical assistance and direct investments. The inter-war period revealed a divide between the aggressive multinational expansion of Goodyear and Firestone through wholly owned subsidiaries and the greater preference of U.S. Rubber, Goodrich, and General Tire for limited investments or technical assistance contracts.

Unlike the expansion during World War I, U.S. tire exports and foreign sales organizations contracted between 1941 and 1945. Goodyear's Java factory was occupied by the Japanese. The Austrian firm Semperit subsequently lost factories in Czechoslovakia and Yugoslavia. There were new wartime investments by Goodyear in Peru and by General Tire in Venezuela and Chile.

After 1945 multinational activity resumed on a grand scale, with an increasing emphasis on less-developed countries. There were 89 new international ventures between 1946 and 1975, of which two-thirds were in developing countries. West picks out two trends. First, American multinational producers extended their interests in Europe. U.S. Rubber broadened its overseas base by acquiring stock in North British Rubber and Englebert (Belgium), and it later took full control of these firms. General Tire opened factories in Portugal, Spain, and Holland, while Seiberling invested in an Italian business. Goodyear built plants in France (1959) and Italy (1963); in Germany it acquired the Fulda company in 1961 before constructing a new tire factory four years later. Goodyear had established a research center in Luxembourg in 1957.

The second trend was investment in Asian and African markets in response to protectionism and the efforts of national governments to promote foreign investments in manufacturing industry. Goodyear, Firestone, Dunlop, and Pirelli were particularly active in these areas. Such protected markets often yielded considerable market power and, since they lagged in terms of product innovation, proved a highly profitable means of maximizing returns from well-established technology. Radial tires, expensive and less suited to poor roads, came late to the developing countries. In some cases developing countries encouraged their own national firms, and this ensured the continuing importance of technical assistance agreements with American and European manufacturers.

Tariffs and oligopolistic rivalry explain the pre-1939 growth of overseas manufacturing when American producers had possessed advantages in tire design and manufacturing methods. U.S. tire imports were negligible, and Dunlop was the only foreign rival to sustain an American factory. However, new and increasingly significant elements came into play after 1950. On the one hand, automobile production and use expanded faster overseas than in the United States. From 1930 to 1950 around 80 percent of world car output was in the United States, but the proportion had fallen to 50 percent in 1960 and 21 percent by 1980. Such shifts explain the pace of overseas investment and the importance to profits and sales of foreign subsidiaries. However, the changes also benefited rival multinationals and brought new competitors to the fore.

The major feature was the spectacular expansion of Japanese automobile production. The Japanese rubber industry was pulled along in the wake of Nissan, Toyota, and others. Bridgestone, a general rubber company established in 1931, emerged as the major tire firm. There were several smaller Japanese tire companies, notably Sumitomo, which had originated as Dunlop's 1909 investment and retained technical links with the British firm, and Yokohama Rubber, in which Goodrich had held a stake. The Japanese firms entered technical assistance agreements; Bridgestone, for example, received technical assistance from Goodyear and supplied tires to Nippon Goodyear, a marketing subsidiary. However, U.S. minority shareholdings declined in the 1980s, and no American firms had their own factories in Japan.

The particular nature of the Japanese car industry created a tire market that was dominated by OE business. When Japanese automobiles began to penetrate export markets, Bridgestone and Sumitomo were brought into the international tire industry through exports and then in the 1980s by direct investment. Japanese imports accounted for 25 percent of the U.S. automobile market by 1985, which represented a large quantity of OE business beyond the reach of U.S. firms. Both Bridgestone and Sumitomo initially created U.S. sales organizations for truck tires and concentrated on California, but by the 1980s Bridgestone's ability to finance modernization and its signs of superior efficiency posed a fundamental challenge to the U.S. industry.

The second new feature was the switch to radial tires, which occurred gradually in Europe after 1950, but suddenly and convulsively in the United States after 1970. Michelin, Pirelli, and other European producers were superior in radial technology to American firms, which were initially hesitant. During the 1960s, Michelin, Pirelli, and Continental all began marketing radials in the United States, often for use on imported European cars. Consequently, when higher oil prices persuaded General Motors and Ford to accelerate the adoption of radial tires, overseas firms, particularly Michelin, took advantage of the American manufacturers' lack of preparation. Michelin increased its imports, built a Canadian plant, and then reentered the American market by constructing a factory in 1976.

The recessions of the 1970s and early 1980s brought together twin pressures on the American multinationals. Japanese imports of cars and tires increased and Michelin expanded its OE and replacement market shares, while depressed demand and poor returns constrained the U.S. firms' ability to modernize. At the same time recessions overseas weakened their foreign subsidiaries, intensified international rivalry, and resulted in a major reorganization of the U.S. and world tire industry in the 1980s.

U.S. multinationals retreated between 1975 and 1984. Firestone closed several overseas plants and concentrated its European production in Spain, while Goodrich and General Tire abandoned manufacturing in Europe, Uniroyal sold its British and Belgian tire operations to Continental. Goodyear closed some plants, but retained a stronger presence. West notes the American firms' increasing acceptance of minority-owned ventures and technical assistance agreements. Meanwhile Bridgestone had established four factories in less-developed countries by 1979, and Michelin was continuing to make inroads into the U.S. market. Within Europe there were some joint ventures: Dunlop and Pirelli participated in a union between 1971 and 1981, and Kleber-Colombes (France) and Semperit operated a joint holding company to cooperate on production, marketing, and research between 1973 and 1979. Both alliances foundered in the face of recessions and losses in the European industry, and several smaller producers were absorbed by multinationals in the early 1980s. In 1985 financial problems resulted in Dunlop's parent company being taken over by British Tyre and Rubber (BTR), a smaller British conglomerate, which had originated as a subsidiary of Goodrich in the 1920s. The bulk of Dunlop's European tire operations had already been resold in 1984 to Sumitomo, the second-ranked Japanese tire company. BTR sold the American division, Dunlop Tire, in 1985, and it became an independent firm. By 1989 Michelin had acquired Kleber-Colombes and Continental had purchased Semperit, while Scandinavian firms Viking and Gislaved merged in 1989 as a defense against acquisition.

Further changes within the U.S. were wrought by foreign manufacturers. The dampening effect of radials on demand began earlier overseas. The international recessions in 1979–80 and 1982 triggered problems of excess capacity, plant closures, and poor returns similar to those in the U.S. As the world's largest tire market with 38 percent of total output, the U.S. held clear attractions, and the foreign manufacturers' advantage in radial technology provided the opportunity for entry, initially through imports. Michelin reportedly accepted low profit margins and enormous losses in order to establish a leading position in the U.S. market. The success of imported cars and the decisions by Honda, Volkswagen, and Nissan to open American factories encouraged their OE suppliers to expand in the U.S. In 1987 GenCorp sold its General Tire division to Continental; General Tire had previously manufactured radials for Continental's U.S. marketing subsidiary, and the German firm had earlier used acquisitions, including of Uniroyal's foreign subsidiaries, to expand in Europe. More dramatically, in 1988 Firestone announced plans to sell its tire division to Bridgestone, the leading Japanese producer, which had entered the U.S. by purchasing a truck tire plant from Firestone in 1983. Initially Firestone was to continue as an automotive supplies business, but Pirelli, the Italian firm, made a counteroffer for the whole company, and Bridgestone responded by acquiring Firestone completely for $2.6 billion. Pirelli, which had also failed in a bid for General Tire, then purchased Armtek's tire division. The strategy of acquisition provided established factories, work forces, and distribution systems, although the transfer to foreign ownership was not entirely smooth: General Motors threatened to drop Firestone as an OE supplier by 1990 following its purchase by Bridgestone. The reorganization was taken a step further in 1989 with Michelin's announcement of its intention to acquire UGTC. The plan offered Michelin a broader spread of brands and prices as well as additional strength in the OE and private brand markets. It also acknowledged UGTC's inability to overcome its debt burden or its early managerial weaknesses. The dramatic changes left Goodyear as the only major U.S.-owned tire producer.

Goodyear remained dominant in the United States, but it entered a phase of clear international rivalry with Michelin and Bridgestone. Pirelli, Continental, Dunlop, and Sumitomo occupied the second rank of global tire producers. The remaining independent tire companies held specialized market niches on the fringes of the industry (see Table 10.1).

Tire manufacturers followed the automobile industry in emphasizing "globalization," namely, the development of a few multinational

Table 10.1. Top Ten Tire Producers
Worldwide, 1988 (%)

Total Sales: $40 billion	
Goodyear	18.3
Michelin	18.1
Bridgestone-Firestone	16.5
Sumitomo-Dunlop	7.5
Pirelli-Armstrong	7.4
Continental-General Tire	6.6
UGTC	4.3
Yokohama	3.7
Other Firms	17.6

Source: *Tire Business,* 1988 World Tire Report.

corporations operating in all markets and marketing standard products. The challenge in the industry, as this century ends, is to resolve the existing tension between the desire for volume production and higher profits on specialist tires and to make marketing sense of the national differences in car and tire uses and personal preferences and incomes.

CHRONOLOGY

1839   Charles Goodyear discovers the process of vulcanization.

1844   Charles Goodyear patents vulcanization in the United States and licenses manufacturers.

1846   Robert Thomson patents his "aerial wheel," a pneumatic tire design, in Britain.

1865   Goodyear's U.S. patent expires.

1870   Dr. Goodrich moves his small rubber business from New York to Akron, Ohio.

1878   Albert A. Pope initiates production of the "Columbia" bicycle.

1888   John Boyd Dunlop reinvents the pneumatic tire in Dublin.

1892   Charles Ranlett Flint organizes the United States Rubber Company, the rubber footwear trust.

1893   The Duyrea brothers operate a gasoline automobile in the United States for the first time.

1895   Michelin pioneers automobile pneumatic tires in Paris-Bourdeaux race. Hartford Rubber Works supply tires to the Duryea brothers.

1896   Goodrich supplies automobile pneumatic tires to Alexander Winton. Bicycle craze reaches its peak.

1898   Goodyear Tire and Rubber established.

1899   Leading tire and mechanical goods firms combine to form the Rubber Goods Manufacturing Company (RGM).

1900	Firestone Tire and Rubber Company incorporated.
1905	U.S. Rubber acquires RGM.
1906	Firestone contract for Ford Model N triggers the collapse of the Clincher Tire Association.
1908	Ford Model T introduced.
1909	Goodyear Tire and Rubber patents William C. State's "core" tire-building machine.
1910	Record prices for natural rubber stimulate the development of rubber plantations in Southeast Asia.
1912	The addition of carbon black as a strengthener changes the standard color of tires from gray to black. Goodrich and Diamond merge.
1913	Akron rubber industry strike.
1915	General Tire and Rubber incorporated.
1916	Goodyear becomes the leading tire producer. Banbury Internal Mixer patented.
1919	Number of tire manufacturers reaches its peak. U.S. Rubber patents "drum" tire-building machine.
1920	In response to postwar recession Firestone cuts prices by 25 percent.
1921	Dillon, Read's refinancing averts Goodyear's bankruptcy, but Frank and Charles Seiberling resign.
1922	British Stevenson Act restricts rubber exports.
1924	Advent of low-pressure "balloon" cord tires.
1926	Goodyear and Sears, Roebuck sign major private brand contract. Firestone embarks on retail stores program.
1927	DuPont obtains control of U.S. Rubber.
1928–29	Rubber Institute fails to achieve industry agreement on prices and trade practices.
1929	Oil companies enter tire retailing.
1930	Michelin closes U.S. factory.
1933	NRA Tire Code signed. I. G. Farben develops Buna-S synthetic rubber in Germany.

1936	Goodyear and Sears contract ends following Federal Trade Commission order and Robinson-Patman Act. "Sit-down" strikes in Akron.
1940	Federal control of natural rubber stockpile begins.
1941	United States enters war.
1942	Japanese cut off Southeast Asian rubber supplies. Tire rationing introduced and progressively tightened. Gasoline rationing established to conserve tires. Gillette Hearings held and Baruch Committee formed. Federal government accelerates synthetic rubber program.
1948	Michelin patents radial tire. Goodrich produces tubeless tire.
1950–53	Rubber consumption restricted during Korean War.
1953	Rubber Producing Facilities Disposal Act enacted.
1955	Sale of federal synthetic rubber industry to tire, oil, and chemical firms. Postwar boom in new car sales reaches its peak.
1961	Firestone purchases Dayton's tire division.
1964	Firestone purchases Seiberling's tire division.
1965	Goodyear purchases Lee's tire division.
1966	National Traffic and Motor Vehicle Safety Act includes federal regulation of tire standards. Bias-belted tire displaces bias tire, but United States lags in radial technology compared with Europe.
1973–74	OPEC oil price increases lead to reduced motoring and reduction in U.S. speed limit. Car firms switch to radial tires.
1976	Michelin opens South Carolina plant.
1978	Recall of Firestone "500" steel-belted radial.
1979	Mansfield quits tire industry.
1980	Federal grading established for radial tires.
1986	Goodrich and Uniroyal merge their tire divisions into the Uniroyal-Goodrich Tire Company; Goodrich sell its share in 1987.
1987	General Tire sold to Continental Tire of Germany.

1988   Firestone acquired by Bridgestone of Japan. Pirelli
          buys Armtek's tire division.

1989   Michelin agrees to purchase the Uniroyal-
          Goodrich Tire Company.

BIBLIOGRAPHIC ESSAY

THE SECONDARY LITERATURE ON THE TIRE industry is limited compared with that on the automobile and is particularly thin on events after 1945. Most aspects of the industry's development would benefit from closer scholarly scrutiny. The principal studies have been company histories of Goodyear, Firestone, and U.S. Rubber, which trace the fortunes of these leading firms. Still, the activities of the majority of firms, large and small, remain poorly documented. A mine of valuable information, particularly on new technology, is contained in various trade journals. For the early period the *India Rubber World*, first published in 1889, is essential, while the *India Rubber Review*, published in Akron, is rather more detailed on the city's firms. The *India Rubber Review* continued as the *India Rubber and Tire Review* between 1926–34 and then as *Tire Review*. The post-1945 period is described and analyzed in journals such as *Elastomerics, Modern Tire Dealer, Rubber and Plastics News*, and *Tire Business*. In August 1988 *Tire Business* published an excellent and well-illustrated commemorative issue celebrating 100 years of the pneumatic tire industry. It is a valuable survey of many aspects of the industry.

Studies of the automobile industry rarely discuss tires directly, but John B. Rae's *The American Automobile Industry* supplies a concise and highly informative overview of the changing character of the tire manufacturers' major customer.

1. The Nineteenth-Century Rubber Industry

Most studies of the tire industry summarize its nineteenth-century origins. Basic information on early rubber manufacturing in Europe and America is contained in Philip Schidrowitz and T. R. Dawson, *History of the Rubber Industry*. A detailed account of the American industry's early development, particularly the formation of the two trusts, U.S. Rubber and the Rubber Goods Manufacturing Company, in the 1890s is provided in Glenn D. Babcock's *History of the United States Rubber Company.* The Baker Library's Manuscript Division has a small amount of material on U.S. Rubber, and its holdings of R. G. Dun credit ledgers have a little information on Goodrich and New York Belting and Packing. My account of Goodrich's activities relies heavily on an unpublished manuscript, "A History of and Statistics Appertaining to the B. F. Goodrich Company for Forty Years from 1870 to 1910" by P. W. Leavitt, the firm's secretary. The manuscript is in the B. F. Goodrich collection in the University of Akron archives. The formation of Goodyear is outlined in two company-sponsored histories, Hugh Allen's *The House of Goodyear* and Maurice O'Reilly's *The Goodyear Story.*

The best account of the bicycle industry is Norman L. Dunham "The Bicycle Era in American History," an unpublished doctoral thesis. David A. Hounshell, *From the American System to Mass Production, 1800–1932,* places the technology of bicycle production and design in a broader context. Changes in tire design and the principal solid and pneumatic tire patents are discussed in Eric Thompkins's *The History of the Pneumatic Tyre* and Walter E. Burton's *The Story of Tire Beads and Tires.*

2. The Beginning of the Automobile Era, 1900–1909

The expansion of automobile production and use, which transformed the rubber industry, is documented very fully in James J. Flink, *America Adopts the Automobile, 1895–1910.* John B. Rae, *American Automobile Manufacturers: The First Forty Years,* gives more information on early firms and entrepreneurs. For the tire industry itself there is a colorful account in Howard and Ralph Wolf, *Rubber: A Story of Glory and Greed,* and useful material in the Goodyear company histories.

The papers of Goodyear's founder Frank A. Seiberling provide further insights into the firm's early growth, its financial uncertainties, and the patent pools. Seiberling's papers (collection 347) are held at the Ohio Historical Society's Library, Columbus, Ohio. Babcock's study of U.S. Rubber describes the footwear firm's entry into tire production through the acquisition of the Rubber Goods Manufacturing Company. In 1951 Alfred Lief detailed the beginnings of another key firm in *The Firestone Story* and supplied a biography of the firm's dominant personality in *Harvey S. Firestone: Free Man of Enterprise.* Lief's studies were supported by the firm and made effective use of Harvey Firestone's personal correspondence, but the recent deposit of Firestone records in the University of Akron's archives may permit a new assessment of the firm's policies and the role of other executives. The emergence of Akron as the center of tire manufacture is traced in Hugh Allen's *Rubber's Home Town,* Karl Grismer's *Akron and Summit County,* and Carl Wittke, ed., *The History of the State of Ohio.*

3. The Emergence of Mass Production, 1909–1916

The merits of Goodyear and Firestone are well rehearsed in their respective company histories, and Babcock ably assesses U.S. Rubber's mixed fortunes after 1909. Alfred D. Chandler has set these firms within the general pattern of changes in the organization and policies of American business in his *Strategy and Structure* and *The Visible Hand*. My article "Manufacturing and Marketing: Vertical Integration in the U.S. Tire Industry, 1890s–1980s" comments on one aspect of Chandler's analysis. Unfortunately, the sparse information on Goodrich, Akron's largest firm to 1909, and Diamond Rubber leaves many issues regarding business strategies unresolved. The formation of General Tire is described by Denis J. O'Neill, *A Whale of a Territory*, which is sadly the only account of this important firm and the role of the O'Neil family, its owners.

Trade journals supply a technical guide to the new tire-building machines and, with the *Akron Beacon Journal*, summarize the events of the 1913 Akron strike. The industry's labor-management relations have been rescued from obscurity in recent years through several fine articles by Daniel Nelson. Goodyear's welfare program and novel form of labor representation were the subject of Nelson's "The Company Union Movement, 1900–1937: A Re-examination," *Business History Review* (Autumn 1982). A broader assessment of the 1913 strike and the development of the tire industry to 1916 is contained in Nelson's book *American Rubber Workers and Organized Labor, 1900–1941*. The social history of Akron remains largely unexplored, although there is material in local directories and Goodyear's house magazine, *The Wingfoot Clan*.

4. Growth and Instability, 1916–1921

The rubber industry's war mobilization can be gauged rather sketchily from secondary sources, but little work has been done on relevant federal sources. The postwar expansion and the subsequent recession feature in company histories. For Goodyear there is additional information from a management survivor in Paul W. Litchfield's autobiography, *My Life as an Industrial Lieutenant*, and some often caustic comments from the principal casualty in the Frank A. Seiberling Papers. Yet there remain gaps in the primary sources on the events of 1920–21. The Frank A. Seiberling Papers are less complete for 1921 than any other year, and at the time of my original research the Harvey S. Firestone Papers were also limited for 1921. Let us hope that the recent deposits of company archives at the University of Akron will permit fuller evaluation of the firms' policies and the role of financial institutions in the crisis.

5. Concentration and Competition in the 1920s

The account of the interwar period is based on my article "Structural Change and Competition in the United States Tire Industry, 1920–1937," *Business History Review* (Spring 1986), though I have given more emphasis to the effects of changes in tire design and quality. For statistics on the industry and early assessments of changing conditions, see John D. Gaffey, *The Productivity of Labor in the Rubber Tire Manufacturing Industry*, and Leonard Carlsmith's *The Economic Characteristics of Rubber Tire Production*. The key account of technical change is Boris Stern, "Labor Productivity in the Automobile Tire Industry," U.S. Bureau of Labor Statistics (Bulletin 585, July 1933). The displacement of less skilled labor in the 1920s is emphasised by Nelson, "Mass Production and the U.S. Tire Industry," *Journal of Economic History* (June 1987), who questions the extent and impact of deskilling. The mail-order firms' entry into retailing is described in Boris Emmet and John E. Jeuck, *Catalogues and Counters: A History of Sears, Roebuck and Company*. Changing conditions in the automobile industry are discussed in Harold G. Vatter, "Closure of Entry in the American Automobile Industry," *Oxford Economic Papers* (October 1952).

6. The Industry in Depression, 1929–1940

The Federal Trade Commission's extensive hearings on the Goodyear-Sears contract are a mine of information, often highly partisan, on the marketing policies and business rivalries in the tire trade during the late 1920s and early 1930s. The records of the various tire industry codes in the archives of the National Recovery Administration's records (RG 9) are also highly valuable. An astute contemporary evaluation is Lloyd G. Reynolds, "Competition in the Rubber Tire Industry," *American Economic Review* (September 1938). Lief and Babcock summarize the responses of Firestone and U.S. Rubber, respectively, to the depression. The Goodyear company histories are less detailed, and the fortunes of General Tire, Fisk, and middling firms such as Kelly-Springfield and Seiberling Rubber all deserve closer scrutiny. An good account of the impact of the depression on one small firm is Ernest B. Fricke, "The New Deal and the Modernization of Small Business: The McCreary Tire and Rubber Company, 1930–1940," *Business History Review* (Winter 1982). A study of McCreary's subsequent history would be well worthwhile. The authoritative source on the era's labor relations is Nelson's *American Rubber Workers and Organized Labor, 1900–1941*. A fascinating new discussion, stressing the differing responses to unions and their limited gains in the 1930s, is Nelson, "Managers and Non-union Workers in the Rubber Industry: Union Avoidance Strategies in the 1930s," *Industrial and Labor Relations Review* (October 1989).

7. World War II

The basic information on complex issues involved in the creation of the synthetic rubber industry is summarized from federal sources by Vernon Herbert and Attilio Bisio, *Synthetic Rubber: A Project That Had to Succeed.* A little more detail on the hesitation, confusion, and animosity that characterized the early stages of the government's rubber supply policies is supplied in William M. Tuttle, "The Birth of an Industry: The Synthetic Rubber 'Mess' in World War II," *Technology and Culture* (1981). Davis R. B. Ross addresses similar issues with more emphasis on corporate attitudes in "Patents and Bureaucrats: U.S. Synthetic Rubber Development before Pearl Harbor," in Joesph R. Frese and Jacob Judd, eds., *Business and Government: Essays in Twentieth Century Cooperation and Confrontation.* A participant, Standard Oil's Frank A. Howard, recorded his recollections in *Buna Rubber.* The rubber industry's own views and the day-to-day operation of the synthetics plants are revealed in some wartime congressional hearings but are still underresearched. The general context of price control is discussed in Harold G. Vatter, *The U.S. Economy in World War II,* and Hugh Rockoff *Drastic Measures: A History of Wage and Price Control in the United States,* chapters 4 and 5. The tire industry's wartime labor relations and the details of the tire rationing schemes could be explored further through federal records.

8. Reconversion, Synthetic Rubber, and Postwar Prosperity, 1945–1965

The Federal Trade Commission's *Economic Report on the Manufacture and Distribution of Automotive Tires* provides a wide-ranging survey and much statistical material on the industry to 1964 and is an essential source. Unfortunately, I have been unable to locate the original records relating to this investigation. Similar ground between 1959 and 1964 is covered in the hearings and final report by the Senate Select Committee on Small Business in *Studies in Dual Distribution: the Automotive Industry.* The FTC's docket 7505 provides further material on the industry in the 1940s and 1950s.

The supply of company histories virtually dries up after 1945. The only complete discussion is Maurice O'Reilly, *The House of Goodyear.* Lief takes the story of Firestone to 1950, but after that there is no account of this key firm or its executives. The Firestone family remained in control, and a study of the firm's later development would be fascinating. The more diversified business strategies of Goodrich, U.S. Rubber, and General Tire and Armstrong's relationship with Sears, Roebuck would also be interesting topics. There is basic material on all firms in their various annual reports and in the trade press, but the opening of their archives to scholarly research would be a valuable advance. The J. Penfield Seiberling Papers (collection 824 in the Ohio Historical Society) permits study of one middling firm, but other similar firms were absorbed by the industry leaders. Edward O. Lamb's antipathy to the Seiberling family is apparant in his autobiogaphy *No Lamb for Slaughter.* Frank J. Kovac, *Tire Technology,* gives a clear and concise summary of the changes in tire design.

Herbert and Bisio outline the transfer of the federal synthetic rubber industry to private ownership. A fuller survey by Charles F. Phillips, *Competition in the Synthetic Rubber Industry,* assesses the industry's subsequent development. Phillips regarded the synthetic rubber business as "workably competitive" despite the concentration of ownership. An opposing view was advanced by Stanley E. Boyle; for exchanges between Phillips and Boyle see the *Journal of Industrial Economics* (April 1961). A condition of the sale of plants was that the U.S. attorney general should scrutinize competition, and the resulting annual reports from 1956 to 1962 are a good source. General rubber policies are described in annual reports by the secretary of commerce between 1948 and 1954.

9. Radials, Recession, and Reorganization, 1970–1988

The dramatic changes in the tire industry's character and fortunes since 1970 are traced in the various trade journals. An essential guide is the January issue each year of *Modern Tire Dealer,* which is devoted to a thorough statistical summary of all aspects of the tire business. *Modern Tire Dealer* supplies information on numbers of firms and plants; estimated market shares for each firm and retailer; sales by tire design, prices, and the location of plants; and expert analysis of the trends. There is also much of value on firms, technology, and topical issues in the pages of *Tire Business, Rubber and Plastics News,* and *Elastomerics.* Further statistical material and interpretation is provided in the Economist Intelligence Unit's quarterly publication, *Rubber Trends.* The responses of individual firms can be traced from their annual reports, but these leave open many fascinating questions about business strategy.

The best overview and evaluation of the 1970s is J. S. Dick's excellent series of six articles on "How Technological Innovations Have Affected the Tire Industry's Structure," published in *Elastomerics* between September 1980 and February 1981. The articles draw on an M.A. dissertation at the University of Akron. Similar material is used by Charles Jeszeck as background for his assessment of changes in industrial relations in the tire industry. His doctoral thesis on plant dispersion provides a compendium of information, and the central themes are set out in a fine article, "Structural Change in CB: the U.S. Tire Industry," *Industrial Relations* (1986). The combination of Jeszeck's work and Daniel Nelson's analysis of the earlier period provides good material on the industry's labor relations, except in the 1940s.

The issue of tire grading features in trade journals and is mentioned briefly in Ralph Nader's *Unsafe at Any Speed*, which also illustrates the general context. The Firestone 500 case was the subject of congressional hearings and reports, notably "The Safety of the Firestone 500 Steel Belted Radial Tires," Report of the Subcommittee on Oversight and Investigations of the House Committee on Interstate and Foreign Commerce (95th Cong. 2d sess., August 1978). The general role of the new federal agencies in tire regulation surfaces in the trade press but perhaps warrants more detailed evaluation if relevant archives can be found.

10. Multinational Enterprise in the Tire Industry

The development of the natural rubber industry, particularly the establishment of plantations in Southeast Asia, has been the subject of numerous studies. Colin Barlow's *The Natural Rubber Industry* provides economic analysis and discusses the science of rubber-growing, while J. H. Drabble's *Rubber in Malaya, 1876–1922* is a more detailed historical account. A useful recent summary, including a little on the post-1945 era, is Austin Coates's *The Commerce in Rubber*. Most work on the role of U.S. manufacturers has focused on their reactions to the British rubber restrictions in the 1920s. Frank R. Chalk's unpublished doctoral thesis, "The United States and the International Struggle for Rubber, 1914–1941" (University of Wisconsin) is valuable. Harvey S. Firestone's campaign that politicized the rubber restrictions as a threat to U.S. interests is described in Lief's biography and company history. A contemporary expression of Firestone's views is his autobiography written in association with Samuel Crowther in 1926. The general industry response and the involvement of Herbert Hoover, then secretary of commerce, is shown in the House Committee on Interstate and Foreign Commerce, Hearings on Crude Rubber, Coffee, etc. (69th Cong., 1st sess., 1926). The earlier and less-publicized promotion of American plantation ownership by Edgar Davis is highlighted in Babcock's *History of U.S. Rubber*. Goodyear's plantation investments are discussed in M. J. French, "The Emergence of a U.S. Multinational Enterprise: The Goodyear Tire and Rubber Company, 1910–1939," *Economic History Review* (1987).

The historical literature on the international manufacturing activities of tire firms is rather slight, though recent events may provide an impetus for further research. An outstanding study is Peter J. West's *Foreign Investment and Technology Transfer: The Tire Industry in Latin America*, which describes global trends and combines material from interviews and secondary sources in an evaluation of the impact of direct investments in South

America. The tire industry is discussed in the general context of U.S. foreign investment in Mira Wilkins's two volumes, *The Emergence of Multinational Enterprise* and *The Maturing of Multinational Enterprise*. Information on the dramatic sequence of recent multinational acquisitions has been gleaned from trade journals and the press; the industry undoubtedly deserves a place in any analysis of the international challenge to U.S. corporations after 1960.

SELECTED
BIBLIOGRAPHY

Allen, Hugh. *The House of Goodyear: A Story of Rubber and of Modern Business.* New York: Corday & Gross Co., 1937; reprint ed., 1943.

————. *Rubber's Home Town: The Real Life Story of Akron, 1825–1948.* New York: Stratford House, 1948.

Babcock, Glenn D. *History of the United States Rubber Company: A Case Study in Corporate Management.* Bloomington: University of Indiana Press, 1966.

Ball, John M. *Reclaimed Rubber: The Story of an American Raw Material.* New York: Rubber Reclaimers' Association, 1947.

Barlow, Colin. *The Natural Rubber Industry: Its Development, Technology, and Economy in Malaysia.* Oxford: Oxford University Press, 1978.

Beasley, Norman. *Men Working: A Story of the Goodyear Tire and Rubber Company.* New York: Harper & Bros., 1931.

Bernstein, Irving. *A History of the American Worker, 1933–1941: Turbulent Years.* Boston: Houghton Mifflin, 1969.

Bernstein, Michael A. *The Great Depression: Delayed Recovery and Economic Change in America, 1929–1939.* New York: Cambridge University Press, 1987.

Bunting, David. *Statistical View of the Trusts: A Manual of Large American Industrial and Mining Corporations Active Around 1900.* London: Greenwood Press, 1976.

Burton, Walter E. *The Story of Tire Beads and Tires.* New York: McGraw-Hill, 1954.

Carlsmith, Leonard. *The Economic Characteristics of Rubber Tire Production.* New York: Criterion Printing Co., 1934.

Chandler, Alfred D., Jr. "The Emergence of Managerial Capitalism." *Business History Review* 58 (1984): 473–503.

————. *Giant Enterprise: Ford, General Motors, and the Automobile Industry.* New York: Harcourt, Brace & World, 1964.

————. *Strategy and Structure: Chapters in the History of the Industrial Enterprise.* Cambridge, Mass.: MIT Press, 1962.

————. *The Visible Hand: The Managerial Revolution in American Business.* Cambridge, Mass.: Harvard University Press, 1977.

Christie, Clowes M. *Looking to the Stars.* New York: Newcomen Society, 1959.

Clark, Victor S. *History of Manufacturers in the United States, 1860–1914.* Washington, D.C.: Carnegie Institution of Washington, 1929.

Coates, Austin. *The Commerce in Rubber: The First 250 Years.* Oxford: Oxford University Press, 1987.

Collier, Richard M. *The River That God Forgot: The Story of the Amazon Rubber Boom.* London: Collins, 1968.

J. S. Dick, "How Technological Innovations Have Affected the Tire Industry's Structure." *Elastomerics* (September 1980):43–48; (October 1980):36–41; (November, 1980):42–47; (December 1980): 47–52; (January 1981):25–30; (February 1981):42–47.

Donnithorne, Audrey G. *British Rubber Manufacturing: An Economic Study of Innovations.* London: Gerald Duckworth, 1958.

Drabble, J.H. *Rubber in Malaya, 1876–1922: The Genesis of the Industry.* London: Oxford University Press, 1973.

Eastman, Joel W. *Styling vs. Safety: The American Automobile Industry and the Development of Automobile Safety, 1900–1966.* Lenham, Md.: University Press of America, 1984.

Economist Intelligence Unit. *Rubber Trends.* London, 1959–. Quarterly publication.

Elzinga, Kenneth G. "The Robinson-Patman Act: A New Deal for Small Business." In *Regulatory Change in an Atmosphere of Crisis: Current Implications of the Roosevelt Years,* edited by Gary M. Walton, 63–74. New York: Academic Press, 1979.

Elastomerics. Atlanta: Communications Channels Inc.

Emmet, Boris, and Jeuck, John E. *Catalogues and Counters: A History of Sears, Roebuck, and Company.* Chicago: University of Chicago Press, 1950.

Epstein, Ralph C. *The Automobile Industry: Its Economic and Commercial Development.* Chicago: A. W. Shaw Co., 1928.

————. *Concentration and Price Trends in the Rubber Tire Industry, 1930–1947.* Privately printed. Akron: 1949.

Federal Trade Commission. *Economic Report on the Manufacture and Distribution of Automotive Tires.* Washington, D.C.: U.S. Government Printing Office, 1966.

Firestone, Harvey S. with Crowther, Samuel. *Men and Rubber: The Story of Business.* London: William Heinemann, 1926.

Flink, James J. *America Adopts the Automobile, 1895–1910.* Cambridge, Mass.: MIT Press, 1975.

———. *The Car Culture.* Cambridge, Mass.: MIT Press, 1975.

French, M. J. "Manufacturing and Marketing-Vertical Integration in the U.S. Tire Industry, 1890–1980s." *Business and Economic History,* 18 (1989): 178–187.

———. "The Emergence of a U.S. Multinational Enterprise: The Goodyear Tire and Rubber Company, 1910–1939." *Economic History Review,* 2d ser. 40, no. 1 (1987): 64–79.

———. "Structural Change and Competition in the United States Tire Industry, 1920–1937." *Business History Review* 60 (Spring 1986): 28–54.

Fricke, Ernest B. "The New Deal and the Modernization of Small Business: The McCreary Tire and Rubber Company, 1930–1940." *Business History Review* 56 (Winter 1982); 559–76.

Gaffey, John D. *The Productivity of Labor in the Rubber Tire Manufacturing Industry.* New York: Columbia University Press, 1940.

Gettell, Richard. "Changing Competitive Conditions in the Marketing of Tires." *Journal of Marketing* 6 (1941): 112–23.

Goodyear Tire and Rubber Co. *The Story of the Tire.* Akron: Goodyear Tire and Rubber, 1948.

Grismer, Karl H. *Akron and Summit County.* Privately printed. Akron, n.d.

Haynes, William, ed. *American Chemical Industry: The Chemical Companies,* vol. 6. New York: D. Van Nostrand Co., 1949.

Herbert, Vernon and Bisio, Attilio. *Synthetic Rubber: A Project That Had to Succeed.* Westport, Conn.: Greenwood Press, 1985.

Hounshell, David A. *From the American System to Mass Production, 1800–1932: The Development of Manufacturing Technology in the United States.* Baltimore: Johns Hopkins University Press, 1984.

Howard, Frank A. *Buna Rubber.* New York: D. Van Nostrand Co., 1947.

Jeszeck, Charles. "Plant Dispersion and Collective Bargaining in the Rubber Tire Industry." Ph.D. dissertation, University of California, Berkeley, 1982.

———. "Structural Change in CB: The U.S. Tire Industry." *Industrial Relations* 25, no. 3 (1986): 229–47.

Jones, Geoffrey, ed. *British Multinationals: Origins, Management, and Peformance.* Aldershot: Gower, 1986.

Killeffer, David H. *Banbury the Master Mixer: A Biography of Fernley H. Banbury.* New York: Palmerton Publishing Co., 1962.

Kovac, F. J. *Tire Technology*. 5th ed. Akron, Ohio: Goodyear Tire and
        Rubber, 1978.
Lamb, Edward O. *No Lamb for Slaughter*. New York: Harcourt, Brace &
        World, 1963).
Lawrence, James C. *The World's Struggle with Rubber, 1905–1931*. New
        York: Harper & Bro., 1931.
Leigh, Warren W. *Gross Margins and Net Profits of Tire Dealers, 1923–*
        1948. Privately printed. Akron, 1949.
Lewis, Cleona, with Schlotterbeck, Karl T. *America's Stake in International*
        Investments. Washington, D.C.: Institute of Economics, 1938.
Lief, Alfred. *The Firestone Story: A History of the Firestone Tire and*
        Rubber Company. New York: Whittlesey House, 1951.
―――. *Harvey S. Firestone: Free Man of Enterprise*. New York: McGraw-
        Hill, 1951.
Litchfield, Paul W. *Industrial Voyage: My Life as an Industrial Lieutenant*.
        New York: Doubleday & Co., 1954.
MacKenny, Ruth. *Industrial Valley*. New York: Harcourt, Brace, & Co.,
        1939.
Maxim, Percy. *Horseless Carriage Days*. New York: Harper & Bros., 1939.
Modern Tire Dealer. Akron, Ohio: Bill Communications Inc.
Moody, John. *The Truth about the Trusts: A Description and Analysis of*
        the American Trust Movement. New York: Moody Publishing
        Company, 1904.
Nader, Ralph. *Unsafe at Any Speed: The Designed-in Dangers of the*
        American Automobile. New York: Grossman Publishers, 1965.
National Industrial Conference Board. *Rubber Products Industry: A Statis-*
        tical Compendium. New York: NICB, 1959.
Nelson, Daniel. *American Rubber Workers and Organized Labor, 1900–*
        1941. Princeton: Princeton University Press, 1988.
―――. "Managers and Nonunion Workers," *Industrial and Labor Rela-*
        tions Review, (October 1989) 41–52.
―――. "The Company Union Movement, 1900–1937: A Re-examination,"
        Business History Review 56, no. 3 (Autumn 1982): 335–57.
―――. "Origins of the Sit-Down Era: Worker Militancy and Innovation
        in the Rubber Industry, 1934–38," *Labor History* 23, no. 2
        (1982): 198–225.
Nevins, Allan and Hill, Frank E. *Ford: Decline and Rebirth. 1933–1962*.
        New York: Charles Scribner's Sons, 1962.
―――. *Ford: Expansion and Challenge, 1915–1932*. New York: Charles
        Scribner's Sons, 1957.
―――. *Ford: The Times, the Man, and the Company*. New York: Charles
        Scribner's Sons, 1954.
O'Neill, David J. *A Whale of a Territory: The Story of Bill O'Neill*. New
        York: McGraw-Hill, 1966.

O'Reilly, Maurice. *The Goodyear Story.* Elmsford, N.Y.: Benjamin Co., 1983.

Orton, W. "Rubber: A Case Study," *American Economic Review* 17, no. 4 (1927): 617–35.

Overman, W. D. "The Firestone Archives and Library," *American Archivist* 16, no. 4 (1953): 305–9.

Page, Victor M. "Making Pneumatic Tires Now a Science," *New England Journal* (12 December 1908): 2–10.

Perrin, William H., ed. *History of Summit County, with an Outline Sketch of Ohio.* Chicago: Bastin & Battey, 1881.

Phillips, Charles F. *Competition in the Synthetic Rubber Industry.* Chapel Hill: University of North Carolina Press, 1963.

Pound, Arthur. *The Turning Wheel: The Story of General Motors Through Twenty-five Years, 1908–1933.* Garden City, N.Y.: Doubleday, Doran & Co., 1934.

Rae, John G. *The American Automobile Industry.* Boston, Mass.: Twayne Publishers, 1984.

———. *American Automobile Manufacturers: The First Forty Years.* Philadelphia: Chilton Company, 1959.

———. *The Road and the Car in American Life.* Cambridge, Mass.: MIT Press, 1971.

Reynolds, Lloyd G. "Competition in the Rubber Tire Industry," *American Economic Review,* no. 3 (September 1938): 449–68.

Roberts, Harold S. *The Rubber Workers: Labor Organization and Collective Bargaining in the Rubber Industry.* New York: Harper & Bros., 1944.

Rockoff, Hugh. *Drastic Measures: A History of Wage and Price Control in the United States.* London: Cambridge University Press, 1984.

Ross, David R. B. "Patents and Bureaucrats: U.S. Synthetic Rubber Development before Pearl Harbor." In *Business and Government: Essays in Twentieth Century Cooperation and Confrontation,* edited by Joseph R. Frese and Jacob Judd, 118–55. New York: Sleepy Hollow, 1985.

Rubber and Plastics News. Akron, Ohio: Crain Communications Inc.

Rubber Manufacturers' Association. *Rubber Industry Facts.* Washington, D.C.: Management Information Services, 1975.

Scherer, E. M. *Industrial Market Structure and Economic Performance.* Chicago: Rand McNally, 1980.

Sloan, Alfred P., Jr. *My Years with General Motors.* Garden City, N.Y.: Doubleday, 1964.

Smallzried, Kathleen A., and Dorothy J. Roberts. *More Than You Promise: A Business at Work in Society.* New York: Harper & Bros., 1942.

Sobel, Robert. *The Age of Giant Corporations: A Microeconomic History of American Business, 1914–1970*. Westport, Conn.: Greenwood Press, 1972.

Solo, Robert. *Across the High Technology Threshold: The Case of Synthetic Rubber*. Norwood, Pa.: Norwood Editions, 1980.

Thompkins, Eric. *The History of the Pneumatic Tire*. Lavenham, England: Dunlop Archive Project, 1981.

Tire Business. Akron, Ohio: Crain Communications Inc.

Tuttle, William M., Jr. "The Birth of an Industry: The Synthetic Rubber "mess" in World War II," *Technology and Culture*, 22, no. 1 (1981) 35–67.

U.S., Attorney General's Office. *Eighth Report of the Attorney-General on Competition in the Synthetic Rubber Industry*. Washington, D.C.: U.S. Government Printing Office, 1962.

U.S., Congress, Senate, Committee on Small Business, *Studies in Dual Distribution: The Automotive Industry*, Washington, D.C.: U.S. Government Printing Office, 1964.

U.S. Department of Commerce. *Statistical Abstract of the United States*. Washington, D.C.: U.S. Government Printing Office (annual).

U.S., National Recovery Administration. *History of the Code of Fair Competition for the Retail Rubber Tire and Battery Code*, no. 410. Approved Code Histories, Div. of Review. RG9, National Archives. Washington, D.C.

Vatter, Harold G. "Closure of Entry in the American Automobile Industry," *Oxford Economic Papers* 4 (October 1952): 213–34.

———. *The U.S. Economy in World War II*. New York: Columbia University Press, 1985.

Walsh, James A. *The Armstrong Rubber Company: Seventy Years of Progress in the Tire Industry*. New York: Newcomen Society, 1982.

West, Peter J. *Foreign Investment and Technology Transfer: The Tire Industry in Latin America*. Greenwich: Jai Press, 1984.

White, Gerald T. *Billions for Defense: Government Financing by the Defense Plant Corporation during World War Two*. Alabama: University of Alabama Press, 1980.

White, Lawrence J. *The Automobile Industry since 1945*. Cambridge, Mass.: Harvard University Press, 1971.

Wilkins, Mira, and Frank E. Hill. *American Business Abroad: Ford on Six Continents*. Detroit: Wayne State University Press, 1964.

Wilkins, Mira. *The Emergence of Multinational Enterprise: American Business Abroad from the Colonial Era to 1914*. Cambridge, Mass.: Harvard University Press, 1970.

———. *The Maturing of Multinational Enterprise: American Business Abroad from 1914 to 1970*. Cambridge, Mass.: Harvard University Press, 1974.

Wittke, Carl E., ed. *The History of the State of Ohio*. Columbus: Ohio State Archaeological and Historical Society, 1941–43.

Wolf, Howard, and Ralph Wolf. *Rubber: A Story of Glory and Greed*. New York: Covici, Friede, 1936.

Woodruff, William. "Growth of the Rubber Industry of Great Britain and the United States," *Journal of Economic History* 15, no. 4 (1955): 376–91.

INDEX

THE AUTHOR

MICHAEL FRENCH IS A LECTURER IN ECO-
nomic history at the University of Glasgow. He received his Ph.D. in 1985
from Birkbeck College of the University of London and has published articles on the business history of the U.S. and British tire industries. He is
currently working on a study of vertical integration in U.S. manufacturing
industry.